16 STRATEGIES YOU NEED TO KNOW TO PROTECT YOUR BUSINESS FROM HACKERS

LEARN THE STRATEGIES FROM 16 CYBERSECURITY EXPERTS

16 Strategies You Need to Know to Protect Your Business From Hackers

Published by Prominence Publishing,
www.prominencepublishing.com

16 Strategies You Need to Know to Protect Your Business From Hackers -- 1st ed.

ISBN: 978-1-990830-01-3

Contents

Foreword

By Chris Wiser

The trend of cyber crime has reached an all-time high this year, and looking back, I can't say that I am surprised. The number of companies supporting remote workforces has increased substantially since 2020 when the COVID-19 Pandemic devastated many of our communities. Employees working remotely around the world are being exposed more frequently to cyber attacks, exposing substantial gaps in Information Technology and cyber security for most businesses.

Business owners should be concerned about these cyber security gaps as technology advances and cybercriminals are finding new ways to use technology to steal data and assets.

It is more important than ever to ensure that business networks are protected, employees are properly trained to recognize cyber security threats, business security postures are improved, and strong cyber security plans are implemented for all businesses, no matter the size, demographic, or industry.

As cybercriminals continue to evolve and enhance threats, businesses will need to also evolve and increase security measures to not only safeguard business data, but also protect business assets from being stolen or compromised.

All businesses are at risk of cybercrime; therefore, protecting your business from cyber threats is crucial and should be top priority for all business owners now and in the future. Understanding the risks and vulnerabilities present within your business is important in protecting your business assets and safeguarding your data.

According to Cyber security Ventures, in 2021 it was reported that businesses were victim of a cyber attack every 11 minutes; costing businesses over $6 trillion worldwide at the end of 2021.[1]

Cybercrime has become too important of an issue to continue to turn your head and look the other way instead of implementing strong cyber security measures within your business network. The time is now to start taking measures and protecting your business from cyber crime.

Cybersecurity experts have created methods to mitigate cyber attacks and malicious cyber threats and have started helping businesses implement strong security measures to protect and mitigate cyber threats. In this book, we have brought together 16 cyber security experts to help business owners understand WHY cyber security is crucial and how your business can stay protected from cyber crime.

You will learn what you can do now to start protecting your business data and assets from cybercriminals and how to start implementing security measures in your business.

Chris Wiser, CEO, 7 Figure MSP

Speaker/Trainer/ Entrepreneur Coach

Cyber Security First: Choosing a Next-Gen IT Firm

By Zach Skagen

Your company's cyber security posture may not be what it seems. More often than not, businesses, both big and small, have to find out the hard way. Well-intended, budget-based decisions end up costing significant amounts of money and harm the company's preciously established reputation and goodwill with its clients and customers. Looking at just 2020-2021, some major companies (4 predominantly) stand out: SolarWinds, SITA, Facebook, and T-Mobile. They all suffered significant data breaches. If these big enterprises, with their major cyber security investments and promises, can fall prey to malicious hackers, imagine the damage that bad actors can do to smaller enterprises through ransomware, phishing, spoofing[2], clickjacking[3], and sniffing[4].

Cyber criminals have historically taken pride in disturbing an organization's IT infrastructure, but more increasingly, their attacks on digital supply chains actually provide a high return on their investment. If companies remain vulnerable to these outside influences due to a lack of next-gen cyber security planning, it is a matter of when – not if – one or more costly data breaches upends the inner workings of those businesses. Holistically, organizations must adopt a *backward design* for their cyber security: First, a complete list of desired IT results must be identified; second, research-based evidence and consultations must drive decision-making processes, not bottom-line; and last, a comprehensive plan must be built on the foundation of risk-mitigation using expertly progressive vision.

The solution to the problem of vulnerable network systems can be complex, depending on existing structures and practices. It is not sufficient for Chief Information Security Officers (CISOs) to rely on their own limited staff anymore. Building and sustaining a constantly evolving infrastructure of security systems requires independent 3rd-party advisement (and often implementation of solutions) from a next-generation IT and cyber security firm with unlimited and unhindered access to the entire IT infrastructure and data. Problems must be identified before they occur. Ultimately, a Cyber Security Mesh Architecture, or CSMA, will consolidate integrated security policies, predicted workflow, and secure data assets. A premier forward-thinking IT firm will deliver their services with the following components guiding their change and evolution: Digital Risk Protection Services (DRPS), External Attack Surface Management Technologies (EASMT), and Cyber Asset Attack Surface Management (CAASM).

With the progressive implementation of cyber security that only a next-gen IT company can provide, existing conventional laissez-faire systems and operations, which are the most vulnerable to cyber attacks, will be eliminated. In collaboration with an organization's executive management and IT staff, a shared vision needs to form that prioritizes absolute and always-developing best practices that are *ahead* of the conventional mainstream curve in IT. Only then can data breaches, financial damage, and business disruption be minimized as much as possible. In turn, the company can focus on its core activities, services, and sales in order to maximize its profits and scale.

With increased vigilance comes conditions that are preceded by the questions: 'Who is in charge?' and 'What exactly needs to be changed?' The in-house IT department can make recommendations or requests for new hardware and software, look for ways to maximize efficiency through new vendors, resolve common helpdesk requests, and perform office moves and installations, which are all examples of first-order change. Second-order change, however, comes about when the new equipment or software, in all its aspects, proves to be more than just "stuff" and embeds effective change relative to a company's long-term vision. The implications of any change in IT infrastructure, policies, and budget must always be beneficial to the efficiency with which a company does business.

Science and technology continue to exponentially evolve year-over-year. Unfortunately, a *vast* number of IT Managed Service Providers (MSPs) are stuck in legacy models of business, which creates immense risk for themselves and their clients – even sometimes being the very attack vector through which a company is breached or ransomwared. These "legacy" MSPs would never refer to themselves as such. However, they should be considered as such because they only apply short-term first-order solutions. They are caught up in the "busy work" of IT. Their apparent 'incompetence' is often caused by limited budgets that are driven by decision-makers higher up in the chain. This makes it difficult for these MSPs to focus on research and development, or to invest in continuing education. Transitioning to new cutting-edge toolsets as they become available is made impossible because the company is too focused on maximizing profit and minimizing tool-spend. Rather than specializing, outsourcing, and *expanding* their service solution to add additional layers of defense and optimization, these MSPs attempt to keep things in-house, *shrink* their service solution, and choose cheaper and less effective vendors. They operate complacently and ineffectively. They experience high turnover with their employees & clients and are constantly fearful of losing their existing clientele if they raise rates (or offer an entirely new, and substantially costlier, solution). They operate at very thin margins and at times, their bottom-line and payroll will be negligently prioritized above all else (e.g., securing their clients' networks, switching to a better vendor, etc.). To lose just a single big client would be significantly detrimental – especially with rising employee salaries and other internal operational expenses. They also know a potentially more negligent MSP competitor can win their client over solely based on price (sometimes by offering a *much* lower monthly rate). So, the 'race to the bottom' continues, and a lot of security risk goes unchecked. Things must change or these MSPs will continue to jeopardize many unaware businesses.

To establish proper support systems that are compatible with the increasingly rising risk, internal IT departments and companies require independent audits by an outside cyber security firm. These firms can uncover deficiencies, blatant and hidden security risks, and a wide variety of things that may be viewed as 'negligence' by insurance carriers, regulatory bodies, governments, and customers. This third-party accountability screening and mitigation plan must also aim to qualify all cyber liability insurance policy mandates. Companies must be certain that in case of a submitted insurance claim, the insurance carrier will not conveniently fall back on any number of *negligence exclusions* in their policy text. Prioritizing high standards, transparent proactive practices, and a continuous assessment of IT competencies (with training & correction) are prerequisites for cyber security risk-mitigation. It is arguable that it is no longer sufficient for *any* company to go about the task alone.

IT MSPs of the future have intentionally chosen to *transcend* conventional wisdom and have adopted progressive, ever-evolving, solutions-based thinking models. Without this new mindset and without proper financial investment, a firm undoubtedly increases its (and its client's) liability. If a *true* cyber security plan is being impersonated by a plan from a negligent MSP with only one or two low-budget tools or vendors, often bundled without any access privilege segregation through their

Remote Monitoring and Management tool (RMM), then this opens the floodgates for bad actors. Additionally, if a firm does not know how exploitable its employees are (possibly due to the increasing strain of cost of living with stagnant salaries), then perhaps even its own network engineers and support staff may succumb to bribes leading to ransomware attacks and other corporate espionage against their clients or their firm. Additionally, retaining their employees is essential in other ways. Low margins (which directly correlate with low wages for the firm's staff), heavy workloads, and stress all lead to high staff turnover, low morale, poor support experiences, lack of change management, and slow helpdesk response times.

Deliberate & progressive investments in cyber security services delivered by a 3rd-party next-generation IT MSP lessens the organizational and administrative overhead for any business, big or small. Currently, 80-85% of organizations – for-profit as well as non-profit – lack investments in proportion to potential data breaches and overall profits. Security-technology convergence is accelerating, driven by the need to reduce complexity, reduce administrative overhead and increase effectiveness. New platform approaches such as Extended Detection and Response (XDR), Security Service Edge (SSE), Zero Trust Network Access (ZTNA), and Cloud Native Application Protection Platforms (CNAPP) are accelerating the benefits of converged solutions.

Successful outcomes of IT decisions depend on the highest levels of consistency and transparency. This involves the third-party next-gen MSP having uncompromised access to systems, data, decision-making processes, and IT budgets. By granting access, the firm can mesh existing and new infrastructures as well as its role with those of the existing IT department, other employees, and different layers of management. This cyber security acumen provides peace of mind. Because of maximized, proactive, and progressive risk-mitigation, it constitutes a high return on investment, since cyber security breaches have proven to be much more costly than paying for the frontloading of next-gen know-how.

If a company sticks with its conventional security and risk management (or no security and no risk management), the cyber attacks against it will be more than just possible threats; they will become real pain and loss. As an organizations' digital footprint expands, strategies against emerging threats must evolve without delay. "Organizations worldwide are facing sophisticated ransomware, attacks on the digital supply chain and deeply embedded vulnerabilities," said Peter Firstbrook, VP Analyst at Gartner. "The pandemic accelerated hybrid work and the shift to the cloud, challenging CISOs to secure an increasingly distributed enterprise – all while dealing with a shortage of skilled security staff."

To accomplish complex solutions to complex problems, the relationship between the next-gen client and the next-gen company itself must be based on trust. Lines of communication must be open, access must be unconditional and instant when needed, and the next-gen firm must have the mandate to mesh its tailored IT solutions with any infrastructure layer, making changes as needed – not delivering a one-size-fits all solution. These collaboration and trust mandates are in the best interest of the client company and will trickle down to making the company more competitive in its industry or service sector.

Choose wisely. Do not gravitate toward low-cost providers. There are many pitfalls unrealized at the signing of the contract when partnering with a legacy firm. When looking for a trusted partner in solving your IT issues, make sure they are aiming to lower your cyber security risk first and foremost. Choose a firm that will serve your best interests by implementing solutions that fuel growth, maximize continuity, and enable progression through long-term partnership and advisement. Not all IT companies are cyber security and risk-mitigation companies. Choose the right next-gen company. One that you can trust and one that gives you peace of mind.

If you want to know more, download the free white paper, 5 Risks You Didn't Know Your Business Had: https://ony.st/5-risks.

About the Author

Zach Skagen has bragged and joked that "computers and technology are his 1st language". He has been taking apart, building, and fixing computers and electronics since he was a young boy. At age 13, he began fabricating and re-packaging network cabling in his parents' basement in order to sell it through his online eBay store while he was attending his 7th and 8th grade.

By his final year of his primary public education, he had sacrificed considerable personal time which he invested instead into web design, development, and hosting, Linux and Window Server administration, and network administration and had even developed his own free-lance client base for whom he helped resolve technology issues.

At age 18, he launched a legitimate business entity that has since transformed into a successful IT & Cyber-security company based in Seattle, Washington. He serves small- to medium-sized businesses (SMBs) by assessing their cyber risk and implementing turn-key solutions that enable growth, continuity, and progression through long-term partnership and advisement. His company aims to be ahead of the curve and continually breaks ground in new services and offerings beyond the competition. With a cybersecurity-first mentality and a motto "As IT Advances, So Do We," they ensure your business will have the latest protection methods. They will ensure continuity plans and procedures are in place so that you can minimize loss and maximize uptime. He invites businesses, owners, and decision makers of every sector to educate themselves on the exponentially increasing areas of risk that SMBs are facing. Not all IT companies are Cyber Security & Risk-mitigation companies.

Onyst.IT https://www.onyst.it aims to be ahead of the curve and continually breaks ground in new services and offerings beyond their competition. With a cybersecurity-first mentality and a motto "As IT Advances, So Do We," your business will have the latest protection methods and 24/7 support. Continuity plans and procedures are put in place so that you can minimize loss and maximize uptime. The owner, Zach Skagen, invites all businesses, owners, and decision-makers of every sector to educate themselves on the exponentially increasing areas of risk that SMBs are facing.

Download the free white paper, 5 Risks You Didn't Know Your Business Had: https://ony.st/5-risks.

Which Industries are Most Vulnerable to Cyber Attacks?

By Doug Johnson

The COVID-19 pandemic caused a massive increase in businesses relying on internet usage. As companies transitioned to a remote workforce model, hackers focused their efforts on finding innovative ways to capitalize on new vulnerabilities caused by this shift. The result is that cyber crime has increased by 600% since the beginning of global pandemic.

In today's global digital business environment, all businesses are at risk of cyber attacks. This chapter will focus on small businesses across all industries and the type of threats they are up against. Small businesses cut across every industry: financial, legal, professional services, manufacturing, medical, insurance, and real estate. The SBA reports that small businesses generate 44% of all US Economic activity. This makes small businesses the largest target for cyber crime.

Small Businesses Across All Industries

Most small businesses don't have the resources or expertise to focus on cybersecurity, which makes them an easy target for hacking. 43% of all cyber attacks are focused on small businesses. According to the US National Cyber Security Alliance, 60% of small businesses that suffer a cyber attack go out of business within 6 months.

One of the most common responses I get when talking to small business owners about cyber security is: "We are small and no one would be interested in our data. What value could our data have to a hacker?" In most cases, it's not your data hackers are interested in. Cyber criminals focus on two things:

1. Disrupting your business by blocking access to your data and systems, holding you hostage for a ransom payment.

2. Gaining access to your financial accounts to steal your money using fraudulent funds transfers.

In today's cyber landscape, nearly every business needs experts to help identify and mitigate cyber risks to keep hackers at bay. Our specialty is partnering with small businesses as a managed service provider (MSP) to identify, mitigate and manage cyber security risks.

Ransomware: What's $300K Among Friends?

A few months ago, we had a client come to us with a big issue. This client usually only came to us from time to time for IT support when their internal person needed help on various projects. Our help desk received a call from their internal IT person saying he thought there might be a virus on their servers. The main database server that they used to run their business was not accessible. Many of their users' computers were displaying a ransom warning and the computers that were still working could not open email or any other files. As it turned out, a user in the shipping department had opened an email from UPS and clicked on a link to track a shipment. The email was not legitimate, and the tracking link led the user to install a type of malware virus called ransomware on his computer. Once installed, the ransomware quietly worked in the background to move through the network, computer by computer, until all folders, files, databases, and email for all 65 users were encrypted and could no longer be opened. The entire business operation was effectively shut down.

All the computers displayed a screen stating that the system had been encrypted and the only way to get access to the data was to contact the cyber criminals to request a ransom payment amount. The ransom amount turned out to be $157K, payable in bitcoin within 48 hours or all the company's data would be permanently lost.

The owner of the company made the decision that they would not pay any ransom to cyber criminals. Instead, they would just restore their data from their backup. We were engaged to help and quickly found that the backups had been encrypted by the ransomware and could not be used to restore the system. Now what? Over the next two weeks, we worked together with their internal IT personnel to rebuild the system from the ground up.

They were able to find a 1-year-old copy of their inventory database but could not recover any files, emails, or any other system data. Over the next few months, the client was able to keep the company running by recreating some of the lost data from hard copy paper files. This disruption to their business and the recovery costs nearly put them out of business.

Please take a moment to think about what would happen to *your* company if you were a victim of a ransomware attack. Would your company survive?

Ransomware claims a new victim every 14 seconds. The average payment following a ransomware attack is now north of $300K – up 171%.

Business Continuity Plans: "All of Our Data is Being Backed Up, or So We Thought"

We had been talking to a company in the financial services industry about engaging us to perform a complete cyber risk assessment of their company and computer systems. We had provided them with a proposal several times, but nothing came of it, and they just got too busy to focus on their cyber security. Until one day when we received a panicked call on a Saturday from the office manager stating that they were in real trouble. All their systems had been infected with ransomware and they were unable to access ANY of their computer systems or data. As a financial services company, they were 100% dependent on their systems and data to conduct business. Our first question to them was, "What about your backups?" They proceeded to say their systems were backed up to a second server in a different location, but that server was also infected, and the backups were encrypted as well. Their only option seemed to be to pay a ransom to the cyber criminals for any chance of getting their data back.

Backup technology has evolved far beyond the days of backing up your data to a removable disk or tape drive in your office where someone takes one copy home. It is now crucial that business continuity be considered primary in your backup strategy. How will your business continue to operate if you lose your primary servers and data? Any business continuity plan must include options to provide fast recovery of lost or damaged data files from a local backup source, as well as the ability to recover data and run your servers from the cloud. Your business is at serious risk if you don't have a backup and disaster recovery solution in place that offers recovery from a local device in your office as well as the cloud.

Business Email Compromise: What Do You Mean, I Just Sent $95K to China?

Our help desk received a call from the CFO of an insurance services firm. He told us their bank just called to confirm a wire request to send $95K to a bank in China. They don't do any business with China and certainly did not transfer $95K to a Chinese bank. After some investigation, it turned out they did transfer $95K to a supplier in Mexico. How did this transfer get diverted to China? Someone intercepted an email from their customer in Mexico and changed the ACH account to that of a

Chinese bank. They have been a victim of business email compromise. They were very lucky that the fraudulent wire transfer was stopped by their bank. In most cases, the bank does not stop the transaction and it is impossible to retrieve the funds.

Business email compromise (BEC) is a cyber crime that involves gaining unauthorized access to the email account of someone targeted in the business. The most common targets are C-suite executives and employees in finance roles. Hackers will use social media and internet searches to determine the person in the organization most likely to be handling money transactions. They will then obtain their email password from a variety of different methods such as the dark web, phishing, or working out easy passwords based on information that is publicly available. Once the hackers get access to the target's email account they will review email activity, then create rules to redirect/copy emails without your knowledge. The hacker could be in your email for months just waiting for you or one of your vendors to initiate a financial transaction. The hacker will intercept an email and change the ACH account number, redirecting payments to a different bank account.

The best practice is to verify ALL electronic funds transfers by phone with the receiving party first. Be sure to confirm amounts, and bank routing and account information. We recommend that at least two signatures be required before any electronic funds transfers are sent.

Twenty-three thousand seven hundred seventy-five complaints of BEC were filed with the FBI last year with losses resulting in $1.7 billion.

Password Theft: But I Keep All My Passwords in a Very Safe Place

The owner of a local small business called us recently in a complete and utter panic. She told us that someone had "taken over her life." A hacker had gained access to her master password list that she kept in an Excel file in a "safe place" on her computer. This file had the passwords for ALL their business, personal, financial, and vendor accounts. She went on to say they were locked out of all their bank accounts, credit cards, QuickBooks accounting, vendor, business merchant accounts, VoIP phone system, and their cell phone accounts. The hackers had even transferred their cell phone numbers to a different carrier so they could get access to any 2FA (Two-factor authentication) codes used as a secondary form of authentication for many accounts.

We determined the source of the hack was on her computer. Her computer was infected with a remote access trojan (RAT). RAT software is most commonly installed by clicking a malicious link in an email or on a website. Once installed, it gives the hacker complete remote access to your computer. They can watch what you are doing, record usernames/passwords from websites you visit and look through all your files for the "Holy Grail," a file where you keep all your passwords.

We were able to help them to recover from this nightmare. It took several weeks to regain access to their accounts, change bank and credit card accounts, get new mobile phones, and rebuild the network and computers so they were secure.

You can avoid this scenario by using an online password vault product to manage your passwords.

Cloud Data Security: We are Safe Because We Have Everything in the Cloud

The abundant availability of cloud-based applications and data storage solutions has transformed the way we do business. Gone are the days of storing our files and data on servers in the office and jumping through hoops to gain access to business resources to work remotely. Applications like Office365 email, SharePoint, OneDrive, Dropbox, online banking, online accounting applications, and remote desktops have made the line between working in the office and working from home disappear. Since these cloud applications are always available and managed by the cloud provider, most people don't think much about cloud data security. While cloud application providers do a very good job of managing their security, there are still business risks with having your data in the cloud.

We recently met with a local law firm who had moved "everything" to a cloud desktop provider. They could simply log into a remote desktop from anywhere and work just as they did when their servers and data were in their office. The law firm loved the convenience of their remote desktops, until the cloud provider experienced a significant and prolonged outage due to a ransomware attack. The cloud provider had a complete and total shutdown of their systems that lasted for weeks. This left thousands of their customers "dead in the water." Imagine no email or access to any of your systems for weeks. How would you run your business?

I don't tell this story to say you should not use cloud-based applications in your business. My intent is to demonstrate the importance of backing up your cloud data to an alternate location and creating a business continuity plan in the event of a cloud provider outage.

Inside Cyber Threats: "Our Employees Would Never Do That!"

The weakest link in a company's cyber security is the end user. Almost all employees are well-meaning and try to do the right thing. The problem is that they don't always know what the right thing is unless they have had proper security awareness training. As illustrated by the previous stories, all it takes is someone clicking on a malicious link to bring ransomware into your network or give a hacker access to sensitive data such as email. Security awareness training should, at a minimum, address these three areas:

1. **Phishing emails and how to identify them -** When in doubt, don't open an email or click links, and ask for confirmation from IT support or the person who you think may have sent it to you.

2. **Personal security behavior training** - This teaches your employees how to set secure, complex passwords, not to write passwords on sticky notes, and not to use the same password on multiple sites.

3. **Physical security awareness -** Habits such as logging off, clearing desks at the end of the workday, and locking offices.

Occasionally, there will be a rogue or disgruntled employee who deliberately sabotages your company security. Over the 22 years I have been working in this industry, I have seen far too many deliberate malicious acts by employees. Here are a few stories:

A CPA client called to say that they had just fired their bookkeeper. Now their users were not able to access the accounting system. We found the bookkeeper had reformatted the disk on the computer that was hosting the accounting system on her way out the door. This is willful destruction of company data, and it happens more often than you would expect.

One of our manufacturing clients fired an employee. This employee was still able to access company email on their personal phone and send email messages. The employee sent an email to ALL employees and many customers that was extremely unflattering of the CEO and upper management. This caused a great deal of embarrassment that could have been avoided by terminating access to ALL company systems immediately before an employee is let go.

I have seen sales and marketing people leave a job only to find out later that they took electronic customer lists and sales data with them to their new job with a competitor. It is vital to ensure that these critical systems are secured to prevent improper export and use of company data.

We recommend our clients use a zero-trust approach to their security. This means anyone with access to your systems and data be set up with the minimum access privileges to do their job. Data loss prevention (DLP) systems should be used to prevent and alert when specific types of data are accessed to be exported, copied to a removable drive, transmitted by email, printed, etc. We also recommend the use of acceptable use policies (AUP) for all employees that spell out how your systems and data can be used. In the event of an employee data theft incident, you may have legal recourse against the employee.

What is the Dark Web and Why Should I Care?

The dark web is the hidden group of internet sites only accessible by a specialized web browser. It is used for keeping internet activity anonymous and private, which can be helpful in both legal and illegal applications. While some use it to evade government censorship, it is also used for highly illegal activity, such as the purchase and sale of stolen website and email credentials.

It is important to understand that using the same or similar username and passwords on multiple sites will lead to your information being available to hackers on the dark web. Most commonly, someone will use their company email address and password to access multiple websites. If one of those websites is hacked and the user information is sold on the dark web, your email address/ username and password are available to hackers and can easily be used to against you in a cyber attack.

Cyber security service providers have access to systems that will search the dark web to see if any of your employees' credentials are listed. This is called a "dark web scan." Ask your security professional to provide you with one.

Phishing, Smishing and Vishing... Don't Take the Bait

Phishing is the fraudulent practice of sending emails purporting to be from reputable companies to induce individuals to reveal personal information, such as passwords and credit card numbers.

Chances are high that you have already been a victim of a phishing scam. This is the most common exploit used by cyber criminals to lure you into giving away sensitive personal information. You have seen them: UPS, FedEx, DHL delivery notices, bogus account/password confirmations from Microsoft, Dropbox, AMEX, your bank, Netflix or any number of other well known sites that you may do business with.

Once your credentials are phished, cyber criminals will use them to access your email, bank, credit cards, cloud file storage sites, etc. This gives them the ability to impersonate you online and then commit an unimaginable number of cyber fraud crimes.

Phishing is not only limited to online accounts and email. Cyber criminals are now using these techniques to phish your mobile phone via SMS text and voicemail.

Smishing is the fraudulent practice of sending text messages purporting to be from reputable companies to induce individuals to reveal personal information, such as passwords or credit card numbers.

Vishing is the fraudulent practice of making phone calls or leaving voice messages purporting to be from reputable companies to induce individuals to reveal personal information, such as bank details and credit card numbers.

There are several things you can do to protect yourself from being phished, smished or vished:

1. Use a different password on each account and site that you access. Can't remember all those passwords? Utilize an online password vault.

2. Utilize 2FA (Two-factor authentication; also called MFA) on as many sites as possible. If your username/password is phished, a third piece of data is required, such as a code number sent to you by text, email, mobile phone app, or phone call.

3. Look at emails and text messages very carefully. If you were not expecting the email or text, or if it looks odd, do not open it or click on attachments or links within the email.

What You Don't See WILL Hurt You!

Just because your computer seems to be working fine, it doesn't mean it is. Cyber criminals often lurk in a compromised computer for months observing user activity. They will move from computer to server across your network to find sensitive data and open additional doors for themselves. When you least expect it, they strike. Most security breaches are not detected for months, or even years.

Many new cyber security software products have recently come to market that detect and defeat this hidden hacker behavior. Four of these next-generation cyber security detection and response products are:

1. Endpoint detection and response (EDR) is a next-generation antivirus software installed on your computer or laptop. EDR solutions detect programmatic behavior that is associated with cyber threats and stops them.

2. Zero-trust endpoint solutions work on the premise that only known and approved programs are allowed to run on your computer. Anything not approved is blocked from installing and running.

3. Network segmentation solutions also work on the zero-trust principle and prevent unapproved network access by programs on your computer. Network segmentation is an effective way to prevent ransomware programs from moving laterally from one computer to another across the network.

4. Security operations center, managed detection and response (SOC MDR). One of the newest and most effective cyber security products is a service backed by a team of cyber security experts who work 24/7/365, responding to detected cyber threats in your system. We have found using a SOC service to be one of the most effective ways to combat cyber security breaches.

Cyber Insurance: "My Business Insurance Covers That, Right?"

Your standard business insurance products such as Errors and Omissions and Business Property & Casualty do NOT cover events related to cyber security breaches and cyber crime.

The cyber security landscape is changing so rapidly that it is necessary for every business to carry cyber liability and cyber crime insurance. Operating without cyber insurance is like driving without car insurance.

Cyber insurance companies are now requiring their policyholders to maintain a specific level of cyber security protection, policies, and practices.

Please call your business insurance broker today to get cyber security insurance coverage in place as soon as possible.

How Can I protect My Company from Cyber Attacks?

As cyber attacks become more frequent and aggressive, businesses across all industries must take action to protect their data and digital assets. Here are some tips for your consideration to help protect your organization:

Limit Access to Information

Human error is the number one security threat for businesses. You can reduce your risk by giving your employees access to only the systems and data they need for their specific role.

Perform a Vulnerability Assessment

A cyber vulnerability assessment will review security weaknesses inside of your company and provide recommendations on how to fix them. To find out more about a cyber security assessment for your business, please visit
https://www.cybertrust-it.com/it-services/cybersecurity/.

Train Your Employees

Educating your employees about cyber risks and how to avoid them is crucial. An acceptable user policy (AUP) will provide guidelines on how employees can use and share company data, email, and internet access.

Engage the Services of a Professional Cyber Security Firm

To keep pace with today's cyber landscape, nearly every organization needs the help of experts to secure their data from hackers.

About the Author:

Doug Johnson, CTO of CyberTrust IT Solutions

Doug Johnson's experience in the IT industry spans over 38 years. For the last 22 years, Doug has worked as an IT and security consultant for hundreds of businesses, across multiple industries. Doug is committed to protecting businesses from cyber security threats and educating the business community on cyber security protection and prevention.

Doug founded CyberTrust IT Solutions to help Southern California businesses grow and achieve their goals by leveraging technology. Today, he architects secure managed IT and cloud solutions to simplify technology, increase productivity, and deliver a competitive edge for small companies in the Orange County & Los Angeles metro area.

CyberTrust IT Solutions is focused on helping businesses stay secure and productive. CyberTrust provides a fixed-fee approach to ensure that your network and technology works. CyberTrust provides private and public cloud solutions based on Microsoft Azure technology.

For more information about CyberTrust IT Solutions and how we can help your business with cyber security or IT concerns, please visit https://www.cybertrust-it.com/it-services/cybersecurity/ or email Doug Johnson at: djohnson@cybertrust-it.com.

5 Reasons Why Remote Devices Are at Risk To Hackers

By Joseph Salazar

Did you know that by 2025, *cyber crime will cost the world*[5] ten and a half trillion dollars annually?

The truth about cyber security revolves around human behavior and how we react to stimuli. Those who are hidden in the dark, sordid corners of the internet, identified as cyber attackers, are pretty much well aware of this. They viciously spend tens of thousands of dollars studying the psychology of how to attack companies' weak points. It's just as simple to phish the receptionist as it is to phish the firm's CEO because they're both swamped, dealing with phone calls, employee queries, paperwork, and a variety of other tasks.

However, with the COVID-19 pandemic, releasing the employees from working in-house to working at their homes became necessary. This opened a pandora's box of unforeseen cyber risks. Employees were thrust into utilizing Microsoft 365 and cloud-based programs, leading many businesses to be left unprepared in terms of cyber security. Consequently, cyber attackers took advantage of an excellent opportunity to do what they are experts at, prey on the workforce by executing cyber attacks more feasibly. While employees feel more comfortable and laid back when working remotely because they are at home and have fewer interruptions, they may not have corporate antivirus installed on their personal computers, and may use the same passwords at work and at home, thus allowing potential breaches of security.

Companies may not understand that their weakest link is mobile security. To access a company's network entirely, a cyber criminal only has to break into one unsecured mobile device (phone, laptop, or tablet). Such intrusions may be debilitating to a small business, costing it money, interrupting operations, jeopardizing crucial data assets, and damaging customer relationships. We are well aware that smartphone users tend to spend a good deal of time outside of a secured business network, using the internet from areas other than the workplace or company sites. As a consequence of this increased flexibility, all too many devices are left vulnerable to more sophisticated hacking tactics — especially when enterprise IT departments fail to deploy mobile device security fixes and upgrades.

Nonetheless, there are defensive strategies that might aid in the prevention of cyber attacks. Here are the top five security concerns that teams must address, as well as recommendations for technology and consumer education to keep people and data secure:

1. Permissive Remote Access Policies

Through virtual private networks (VPNs), a cyber attacker could gain access and slice into the remainder of whatever network is left to invade. If we look at the historical use of VPNs, mostly technical employees were the ones who used them to access vital technological assets. In more recent times, however, VPNs are frequently suggested to all users for the sake of having a more secure connection than personal or public networks. Even users who have no use of VPN software have them installed on their devices. Many old firewall rules allow access to almost anything on the network, which is a grave concern. Every now and then, angry former employees use this sort of weakness, and cyber attackers may simply use it as well.

How Can It Be Prevented?

To avoid this situation, businesses must restrict access related to user identity, granting specified groups permission to only the information required to do their tasks and then gradually increase access as needed. Network segmentation and layer 7 firewalls for advanced traffic control, updating internal servers and clients, and employing sophisticated threat prevention capabilities are all necessary ways to limit a cyber attacker's ability to move laterally via the network. Additionally, an antivirus must be installed, especially by those who work remotely, to thwart any exploitation attempts, thus keeping the penetration risk to a minimum.

2. The Dilemma of New Devices to Protect

Many firms have been obliged to purchase and distribute new devices and other gadgets to their increasingly remote workforce as a result of the current global "stay at home" work affair. Some companies enable employees to use their home equipment for professional functions on a temporary basis. Security teams face distinct issues as a result of this growth in new gadgets. It becomes tedious for the teams to make certain that these devices are malware- and virus-free. With a geographically dispersed staff, they need to ensure that security systems can be installed, managed, and supported remotely.

How Can It Be Prevented?

What could be done is to extend endpoint security to all users working remotely. This includes endpoint protection, detection, and response capabilities, if not done previously. Consider cloud-native methods for endpoint and network security, which are built for regionally scattered workforces. Endpoint threats like malware, exploits, and file-devoid assaults should be blocked. But dangerous behaviors like employees utilizing illegal desktop-sharing programs at home must be checked as well. Only trustworthy devices on the corporate network that meet the defined criteria through host information profiles should be permitted.

3. No Checks on Remote User Activity

Because of the pandemic, employees at various companies had to switch to remote working, which was unexpected and unprecedented. For such employees, security teams must now monitor a whole new set of endpoint devices for malware, file-devoid attacks, and a slew of other threats aimed at them. Many security teams lack the required attention to monitor remote user activity and incoming and outgoing traffic within their network, making it impossible to detect sophisticated threats from distant users or notice when an attacker is transferring from a compromised user's workstation to hosts within the network.

To make matters worse, security analysts, like the rest of the workforce, frequently work from home, exacerbating current security operation issues, including maintaining autonomous penetration, systems response, and pivoting console via console to analyze threats. This confluence of issues makes it simpler for cyber opponents to sneak up on companies and launch an assault.

How Can It Be Prevented?

To avoid this issue, I would recommend that companies consider security platforms that enhance system integration, reduce tool switching, and provide insight into all data, including remote user behavior, rather than investing unnecessarily in discrete solutions. With the help of extended detection and response (XDR), endpoints can be protected, and analytics can detect risks of irregular access or lateral movement. Then, investigations can be streamlined through the sewing of data and finding the underlying cause.

4. Users Combining their Personal and Professional Passwords

Users have a nasty tendency to repeatedly use the same password. They are either unaware of or unconcerned about the potential that one of their sites could get hacked. Once the user's password gets released on a site like pastebin.com, the ground is open for cyber attackers to get access to all of their accounts, including their corporate ones. A remote workforce where employees utilize personal devices and networks with far weaker security standards than their corporate-controlled equivalents compounds the problem, making it simple for attackers to access company data.

How Can It Be Prevented?

My recommendation for avoiding this dilemma is to get trained in recognizing phishing attempts. For users working remotely, in-house security teams could focus their efforts in guiding these users on creating strong, unique passwords, especially with the use of a password manager. Client credentials and multi-factor validation must be used to prohibit attackers from gaining access through vulnerable devices.

5. Phishing Effort at Inopportune Times

Phishing is the most common method of gaining access to business networks. By using fear, panic, and haste, cyber attackers attempt to lure their victims into accessing fraudulent websites. The most recent phishing scam is the "memo from HR" in which the users receive an email with a link to a message. When they click on the link, their credentials are taken and later sold. Such emails, with the name of an institution, benefit from the user's sense of urgency to respond. What this means is, the user would be startled to see this email in their inbox and would think of it as extremely important, thus having the urgency to open it quickly.

How Can It Be Prevented?

My recommendation for avoiding this breach of privacy is to make sure you and your employees educate yourselves in detecting such emails — by the nature of their subject lines and the body content of the email itself. Ask: what kind of email says to read an XYZ message and then tells you to open a link to view it, rather than showing the content to you directly? Moreover, if you are working remotely for a firm, you, along with your colleagues, should know how to spot and report suspicious links and emails and be extra cautious with work accounts as well as any personal accounts. Working as an employee for a company and using work email accounts makes users more prone to receiving such fraudulent emails. To assist, prevent, and identify malware, make sure your email security is up-to-date, as well as your endpoints. Additionally,

URL filtering also helps to avoid phishing attempts by blocking access to harmful websites.

Keep Your Business and Workforce Protected

Data security will become even more important as the culture of remote work proceeds as a realistic choice for many firms. It may be just as safe as employees who work onsite behind the high-tech security fences that most companies have in place. You can guarantee that your company's data and systems are secure by identifying the above-listed biggest security problems for remote jobs and making an effort to mitigate them. Employees will then have a better grasp of the hazards and how to safeguard their personal networks and devices when working remotely.

It's absolutely plausible that employees may work from anywhere in today's internet environment, but that doesn't mean companies have to expose their data, information, or systems to danger. Remote employees and enterprises may feel more secure about their remote security with these safeguards in place, and hackers won't be able to exploit them.

About the Author

Joseph Salazar is the Vice President of Operations at Netwiz Computers located in Placentia, CA. He lives nearby in Yorba Linda and has nearly 30 years of experience working in the IT industry. Starting out as a Helpdesk IT Support Technician, Joseph quickly climbed the ranks, gaining industry knowledge with every step he took, leading him to where he is today.

Joseph got into this field because he was fascinated by how important problem solving was in the IT industry and he noticed how solutions were constantly having to adapt to new threats. When several IT firms were hit with ransomware, he spent weeks working intensely with these firms, figuring out how they had been attacked and what they could do to ensure it didn't happen to his clients. He quickly realized it was not just important to find out what caused a cyberattack, but also to figure out how to prevent it from happening in the future. Each day brought a new threat and each day he brought a new solution.

In addition to his role at Netwiz Computers, Joseph also takes pride in being active in his community. He is an active member of the Yorba Linda Chamber and is the President of the Brea Kiwanis Club. They do various fundraisers that help provide assistance to less-fortunate kids in the area. His Kiwanis club also puts on the popular city-wide Spelling Bee, the Essay Contest as well as the Toys for Tots and Easter Egg Hunt providing Toys and Treats for the Children. He also Feeds the Seniors at the Senior center as well as provide free services to wash their Cars and mow their lawns.

As Vice President of Operations for Netwiz Computers, Joseph helps his company serve the Orange County area by providing reliable, consistent, and professional IT services. They have been successful at doing it since 1998. They focus on providing their clients with Enterprise-level services and solutions for small businesses. Time and experience have helped them develop best practices and workflow procedures around a proactive philosophy designed to minimize disruption and keep their clients focused on their business, not their technology.

You can connect with Joseph at:

NetwizComputers.com

joe@netwizcomputers.com

(714) 455-2925

What is the *Internet of Things* and How Does It Affect My Business?

By David Burton and Wes Jensen

The Internet of Things (IoT) is a business trend that has expanded substantially since its inception just over twenty years ago. Although many people have now heard of the IoT and own at least one IoT-enabled device, most know surprisingly little about it. With most businesses now getting on board with the IoT, you may be considering how to employ this trend within your organization. But what do you need to know first? Here, we'll explore the ins and outs of IoT and demonstrate how it may benefit your business.

Everything You Should Know About the IoT Before Hopping on Board

What is the Internet of Things?

The simple explanation of the IoT is that it's a **network of interconnected people and things** collecting and sharing data. It now includes appliances such as refrigerators, car engines, security systems, televisions, and much more.

The Internet of Things has a history going back as far as 1980 when a group of students at Carnegie Melon University used their computer network to program the campus vending machine so it could report on how many cans of Coca-Cola were left. However, it wasn't until 1990 that a device was connected to the internet when John Romkey connected a toaster. The following year, some students at Cambridge University used a webcam to report on the level of coffee in the pot in their lab.

Although IoT was making its debut in these instances, it wasn't until 1999 that the term "Internet of Things" was actually coined by Kevin Ashton, then working at Proctor & Gamble.

By 2000, the concept had caught on with businesses, and it was in this year that LG Electronics introduced its first connected refrigerator. After that, the number of internet-connected devices began to grow exponentially, and experts predict that there will be over 25 billion internet-connected devices by 2030.

The IoT Ecosystem

So now you know what the Internet of Things is, but how does it work, and what are the parts that come together to make it a usable system? Essentially, there are **four main components** that operate together to create the IoT. These are:

1. Hardware
2. Gateways

3. The Cloud
4. Apps

Let's explore each of these components:

Hardware

The hardware that runs the IoT contains **sensors** that measure elements such as motion, temperature, or speed. This can be a motion sensor that detects someone entering a building, a speed sensor measuring the speed of a conveyor on a production line, or an oil level sensor in your car.

This hardware can also **transmit the data** that it gathers, or receive instructions via the internet, using either a hardwired connection or wireless transmission in the form of WiFi, Bluetooth, 5G connectivity, or any other wireless internet protocol.

Gateways

Gateways **bridge the gap** between hardware devices and the internet or interconnected web. They receive the signals from devices, collect the data, and send it on to the internet infrastructure.

The Cloud

The cloud is used for a multitude of tasks these days, from data storage to running software, and enabling work-from-home for people who used to work in offices. As part of the IoT dynamic, the cloud is used to process

data received through gateways and interpret it to make it useful for an end-user.

Apps

Once data has been processed via the cloud, it needs to find its way to the end-user, and this is done via apps. As all of the data has, up to this point, consisted only of ones and zeroes, apps are needed to **process it into a form that humans can understand and react to**. Apps can run on your PC, laptop, smartphone, or even your TV.

These four parts work together, hopefully in a seamless fashion, to help people usefully access the Internet of Things and improve their lives and businesses.

A simple example would be the heating in your home. A temperature sensor transmits information via a gateway, and the cloud processes it and passes it to an app that also connects to your boiler. If the temperature is low, it instructs the boiler to switch on, and if it's too high, it instructs it to switch off. You can access this data using an app on your smartphone that also enables you to set the temperature remotely, and perhaps add timed settings for day and night or even for when you're away on vacation.

How Will the IoT Benefit My Business?

So now that you know how the Internet of Things works, you may have noted some of the benefits of using it in devices around your home. But how can this benefit your business? Well, there are a vast number of ways the IoT can help your business **expand and become more profitable.** Here are just a few examples.

Security and Monitoring

In the past, electronic security systems were bespoke projects, requiring miles of wiring, processing units, expensive cameras, and specialist companies to install it all. Using the IoT, you can purchase cheap webcams, motion sensors, and access control devices that will rely on WiFi to connect via the internet to apps on your PC or smartphone. Then, if you need to add to the system, you simply buy more devices and add them to your app.

Employee Management

The Internet of Things has many possible applications when it comes to managing your staff and improving productivity. Here are a few ideas:

- **Intelligent access control** to monitor employee attendance and hours worked. You could use this to enable flexible working hours. Employees who manage their own hours tend to be happier and more productive.

- **Enable remote working**. Connecting devices together means that your team members don't have to do all of their work from the office. They can perform their work from home or some other location such as a coffee shop or hotel room.

- **Smart devices to improve the work environment**. Some examples include: trash cans that let you know when they need to be emptied, a coffee machine that tells you when to refill it and reorders supplies automatically, and bathrooms that ask to be cleaned. These things may seem like a small matter, but they, too, boost employee morale and lead to a better-maintained environment.

- **Smart speakers and voice-enabled AI**. These devices can give employees access to smart virtual assistants to take on menial office tasks.

Inventory Management

To improve control of inventory, **smart tags** can be attached to stock for recording sales and returns, improving efficiency. This is particularly effective with fast-moving consumer goods, and many companies are already using this technology.

Maintenance

Smart devices can flag when they **require essential maintenance** or when faults have developed. This can be used for machinery within your manufacturing plant and will help to **reduce downtime** through unexpected faults caused by poor maintenance. Consumer goods can also feature smart maintenance and fault recognition applications. The auto industry is already well-advanced in this regard, and home electronics items use the technology extensively.

Reduce Energy Costs

As noted earlier, you can use the IoT to **control heating systems**. As well as in the home, you can employ this technology to reduce energy consumption within your office, factory or commercial space. Additionally, you can use smart sensors to **control lighting**, turning off lights when an area is not in use. Manufacturers can also achieve further energy savings using **smart production lines** to identify areas of low efficiency and suggest improvements.

Risks of Using the IoT

As wide-scale adoption of the IoT is still a relatively new phenomenon, the technology can still be regarded as new so it is poorly understood by many. This means that you need to consider a number of risks and vulnerabilities when thinking of upgrading your business to using the IoT. Consider the following:

Poor Quality Devices

Many off-the-shelf mass-produced IoT devices are available, and the quality is not always perfect. A few issues with devices can be:

- **Passwords** - Often, passwords for devices are weak or hard-coded, leaving them vulnerable to hacking.
- **Hardware issues** - If the hardware itself is not well-made, has poor-quality sensors, or can easily be cut

off from the network, this can be a serious point of failure.

- **Insecure update mechanism** - Most devices require software updates at some point. If this system is insecure, it's vulnerable to hacking, and your whole system can be compromised.
- **Operating systems and software -** If the operating systems are old or haven't been updated, they may not work correctly and may be more vulnerable to hacking.
- **Data transfer and storage** - If the data storage and transfer systems are insecure, your system is again vulnerable.

Insecure Vendor Devices

Issues with devices don't end with ensuring that devices in sensitive areas are quality, secure products. Vendor devices provided by third parties can also be a risk if they're integrated into your network.

A prime example of this is a recent attack on a casino involving a smart thermostat in a fish tank. Hackers accessed this relatively simple device, which was unfortunately on the same network as computers containing the personal information of high-roller clients. The hackers accessed the device, and then the network, and pulled information out of the database — through the thermostat and into the cloud.

An earlier example is a data breach at Target in January 2014. On this occasion, attackers had breached a company that supplied HVAC systems to Target, gaining **vital login details**. The HVAC systems were, unfortunately, not segregated from vital data systems storing payment card data and were then used to obtain sensitive customer data.

The takeaway from this is that businesses need to either consider their IoT networks as a whole and ensure **full security throughout** or ensure that lower priority systems are **fully segregated** from critical systems and databases.

User Knowledge

Even if you have the best, most up-to-date devices, apps and systems, it can all fall apart if you or your staff do not have the knowledge to use them effectively. If **users aren't properly trained**, your organization loses some of the efficiency gains. Additionally, poorly trained users may leave your systems open to cyber attacks.

Botnet Attacks

If one device on your network becomes infected with malware, it won't usually pose a serious problem. However, if a significant percentage of them are infected, this can bring down your entire network. This is because hackers perform botnet attacks by **infecting large numbers of devices** and cause them to make thousands of requests per second, overloading networks.

Ransom demands may accompany this, and this is known as **ransomware**. The latest version of this form of attack is Mozi, which targets IoT devices in particular. In the first half of 2021, Mozi reached 360,000 unique systems from manufacturers, including Huawei, Realtek, and NETGEAR.

Industrial Espionage

Every business that uses the Internet of Things will have enormous amounts of data about their organization stored within their network. This makes it a very tempting target for hackers engaged in industrial espionage. These hackers are usually independent groups aiming to **sell the data** they have gathered. Just like businesses, today's hackers often organize and network; they boast sophisticated operations that have the potential to inflict serious enterprise-level disruptions.

One such example of this is the Russian-speaking RedCurl hacking group, which has been active since at least 2018, attacking at least 14 organizations in 30 separate attacks. The group uses phishing emails to gain access to business networks and steal internal corporate information. The damage and cost of these attacks poses a serious issue for businesses. Not only do they risk financial losses, but also the loss of their customers or clients' trust when data is compromised.

Rogue Devices

With the large numbers of devices active on IoT networks, it has become easier for criminals to introduce rogue devices, which appear to act as the original device but have in reality been placed to **intercept data**. These can take the form of replacement access points, cameras, or thermostats.

Summary of Risks

While all the risks detailed above might seem alarming, they are all avoidable by taking certain precautions. As the IoT grows, so does the knowledge of users and manufacturers of devices. To keep your network secure, remember to:

- Obtain devices from reputable manufacturers
- Keep software up to date
- Ensure users are well-trained
- Use strong passwords
- Be vigilant for rogue devices

Conclusions

According to Fortune Business Insights, the global market for the IoT in **2020 was worth USD 309 billion** and is expected to grow to **USD 1,855 billion by 2028**. The rapid growth and vast size of this market show that the IoT is seen as one of the best ways to **modernize and grow businesses**.

Moreover, with the enormous benefits provided in data gathering, reductions in energy costs, and improved maintenance of machinery of products, most companies and organizations will be keen to get on board with this technology if they haven't already.

However, the IoT is not without its risks, and businesses should adopt with caution. When adopting IoT devices, it's crucial that business leaders **keep up with the technology**, keep staff fully trained, and ensure that the hardware and software are of the highest standard. Once you have come to grips with these lessons and embedded the right culture into your organization, the IoT can benefit almost any business, large or small.

About the Authors

Wes Jensen

Before starting his first IT company in 2001, Wes was the network administrator at the largest K-8 school district in California. Being the only administrator, with the responsibility of managing over 50 locations and thousands of endpoints, he learned to efficiently leverage technology management at scale.

When Wes was introduced to his first small business client, he realized that most companies are either struggling with needless inefficiencies with their computer systems, or even worse, operate in such a way that it puts the survival of the company at risk.

In 2019, David and Wes formed Cyber Security Advisors to enhance the services provided to their clients. Their vision for Cyber Security Advisors is to help businesses reduce their risk and become the most productive and protected in the US.

David Burton

After David Burton graduated with a civil/structural engineering degree, he was challenged with networking five departments together to improve business efficiencies.

Upon successful completion, he was asked to return to his previous role. "No, thank you!" he said.

David had discovered his passion. It was more than improved bottom-line numbers. There was a distinct positive buzz throughout the office. He quit his job, started technology consulting, and never looked back.

Two decades of cybersecurity experience and an MBA has taught David the value of leveraging a strategic approach to technology. David's approach helps clients achieve business resilience by planning for unforeseen events and implementing a framework to minimize downtime.

Interested in partnering with David, Wes, and the team at Cyber Security Advisors? Please contact them at www.CyberSecurityAdvisors.com.

Why Is Cyber Security User Awareness Crucial for My Business?

By Emilio J. Mejia

What do you think is the biggest cybersecurity threat to your business?

Let me give you a hint: it has nothing to do with technology.

If your answer is, "My employees," then you are absolutely correct. The weakest security link in businesses today is the employees with access to information and with little to no knowledge of security awareness and how to identify possible threats.

According to a study by IBM, 95% of breaches are caused by human error so it is crucial that businesses adopt a solution that helps prepare their employees for the ever-changing landscape of cyber threats. The goal should be to train your employees so that the chances of a data breach are significantly reduced. Businesses and individuals should take a proactive approach to security awareness training; once you are compromised it could be too late.

At Prodigy Technology Solutions, we do just that. For our clients, we provide a solution with layered security to help mitigate the risk of attacks and breaches. Our clients have important and sensitive information to protect and we become their strategic partner that ensures all their data stays safe, and their company is in compliance, and is ready to weather the storm in case they are breached.

We make sure that our clients are prioritizing IT security as a whole, but let's shift our focus to our security awareness solution. Prodigy Technology security training is a robust security platform that protects our clients' businesses by providing customized security awareness training, simulated phishing campaigns, detailed security policies, and thorough security risk assessments — all through a single client-branded portal. Prodigy helps businesses of all industries and sizes by working together to close the door on cyber criminal activity.

Why do my users need cyber security training?

Things have changed over the last 2-3 years, and cyber attacks have been on the rise. Companies are at risk of losing personal identification information (PII), intellectual property (IP), their reputation, and even money in most incidents.

Security awareness for users helps your team identify possible threats and encourages a culture of security compliance in your organization. If you know that the biggest threat to your company is your employees, then why don't we start with addressing that very problem?

Even a modest investment in cyber security training has a 72% chance of significantly reducing the business impact of a cyber-attack. There are more components to cyber security awareness training, and I will be touching on those as we move through this chapter.

Why? You don't know what you don't know!

How can an employee look out for a threat that he has never seen, heard about, or even been exposed to? For instance, if a user is never told to have a second form of verification when someone sends a request for a new recipient of a wire transfer, that employee will likely make any change requested by an email that looks legit. Of all attacks, 60% are business email compromise (BEC). This is when a hacker has obtained access to someone's mailbox by one method or another and emailed that person's contacts, posing as the original email sender. They will then ask for money or some type of procedure where the outcome is financial gain and deception.

Enabling your employees to identify possible threats will decrease the likelihood that your business becomes the victim of an effective hack attempt. There is no 100% solution or tool to keep you protected from all cyber threats, but training your team is certainly the first step in mitigating your risk. We can't keep count of the number of businesses that find us after they have been breached, and one of the first questions that we ask is,

"Are your users trained to identify these types of threats?" The answer the majority of the time is, "No, we don't provide any official security awareness training."

In 2020, J.J. White Inc, a large, multi-trade contractor, engaged Prodigy on a co-managed & consulting basis. They wanted Prodigy Technology to consult and recommend solutions for their IT security posture. We immediately analyzed what was missing and recommended starting with the implementation of a security awareness program. Fast forward to a year and a half later: on our platform, there is a vast difference in the visibility into the J.J. White's cyber security vulnerabilities. VP of IT and CIO Jason Morovich says, "We have seen a swing in users' behavior to keep our company data safe, as well as an effort to watch for all possible attacks."

Baseline Security Assessments

We recommend and conduct baseline security assessments for our clients and potential clients. This allows a company to see exactly where their employees stand in terms of knowing how to identify a possible security threat. Once a business has a baseline on their team, they can make better decision around the type of security parameters that they want to implement or the level of employee training needed.

Yearly baseline security assessments help accomplish a couple of things. The first is finding out what the user has learned or improved on over the last year of weekly or monthly trainings. The second is it allows the employer to identify if training needs to change or be tailored to something specific that a larger percentage of employees might be struggling with.

Build-a-Security Awareness Training

You might be asking yourself, "What should my security awareness training consist of?"

Solutions will vary, but your security awareness training should all have a couple of primary things. The first would be that it is ongoing, whether it's weekly or monthly. New cyber attacks come out every day so we want to make sure that users are being updated on new possible threats that they might face. The training should also be current and stay on-trend with real-world cyber security attacks; there is no reason to train your team on something that is outdated. Companies should also have the ability to track the user's engagement with their security training. You want to know who has taken it and who has not. Is there someone with access to high-level information that is ignoring their security training? Your business should have a plan for management or HR to address that.

Prodigy Technology has a robust training platform that includes:

- Annual cyber security assessment (45 min training 1x a year)
- Weekly micro training, 3x month (2–3-minute engaging videos)

    - After each micro training there are four true-or-false questions

- Monthly security newsletter
- Phishing simulation test
- Dark web monitoring

The solution listed above has full reporting and notification capabilities in which we build rules and workflows to help our clients take full advantage of our platform. These tools work together on one platform, allowing for user training, checks and balances, and even monitoring of outside breaches, so that we can become aware of them and take action.

Adoption & Engagement of Security Awareness

Your company decided to make the security-conscious decision of implementing a security awareness program, but now you are not sure how to get your employees to adopt the security practices and engage with the training platform. I tell any client that works with Prodigy Technology Solutions that if the plan is to implement a security training solution, ownership and management must be 100% behind it.

Everyone needs to use the platform no matter how high or low they are on the totem pole. If you have access to the company's resources with your login, then you need to be part of the training solution.

Now how do we get the employees to buy in? Our dashboard shows scores, leaderboards, and nicknames, and allows us to schedule weekly or monthly reports to provide to our clients. Prodigy Tech encourages their clients to "gamify" the training platform. The tools and features are already built into it; the only decision that is needed is what game and what rules.

We advise clients to break the company up into teams. For this example, let's assume it is a company of 50 users. We break them up into five teams of 10 users. The "game" or contest can be monthly or quarterly, and the rules are as follows:

- Each team's points will be tallied at the end of the month and the team with the most points gets a prize. Prizes can range since each business' employees are incentivized differently. Some examples are: a free PTO day, Amazon gift cards, or free lunch/dinner for the winning team.

- Teams will earn points by:

    - Watching their weekly training within the first 48 hours that it's sent out

    - Catching a malicious email and reporting it to IT

    - Catching a phishing test email that IT sends out deliberately and reporting it to IT

    - Various other methods

At the end of the game's cycle, the winning team is rewarded, and the game may begin again. Once users start to catch on to the phishing simulation and training, it is always good to turn up the difficulty of the phishing simulation. An advanced approach that we like to take is to target certain departments. Instead of sending a generic template, we would create a custom template to target the different departments in correlation with what they work with. For instance, the finance department will be targeted with invoicing, financial statements, and other related emails. The shipping department will be targeted with logistics, shipping, and anything that they deal with daily.

Hackers will take their time and do their homework on your company and its employees to make their attacks as efficient and capable as possible.

Creating teams allows the members to keep the team in check. Employees want to strive for the prize so if someone on their team is not keeping up with their training, they have their peers pushing them. Most employees will be motivated by winning a prize, but unfortunately there are always employees that will only do it if there are repercussions to not participating. Each company can work with their HR department to come up with a suitable policy for employee trainings.

There are plenty of "gamification" ideas; each company will have to assess what fits their employees and company culture best.

Things to avoid when implementing security awareness training

A lot has been covered, and before sending you off on your cyber security awareness journey, we should touch on some things to avoid when implementing a security training solution in your company.

One-time training methods:

"Emilio, can't I just send my users an email once a week or every month with a security tip?" You ask.

Yes, you can. The question is, how effective will that be? How do you know who opened and digested the email? How do you know that they will put it into practice?

With one-time training methods, there is no continuation. It will not spark a conversation in the lunchroom every week and cyber threats are continuously evolving. There is no way to get all the information that users should know into a 45-minute to one-hour session. Therefore, a good strategy is to send the employees 2-5 minute videos at a time and keep them consistent.

Lack of expertise or exposure:

Who is choosing what to send to the employees? Is this person qualified to make those decisions? Is this person exposed to the security world and do they know what trends to stay on top of and what content to deliver?

They don't need to be the highest-level security expert, but it should not be someone in HR who provides training videos on other subjects.

No Tracking and/or Accountability:

Not knowing who is taking courses or failing phishing simulations is almost as bad as not having a security awareness program in general. If you are implementing a system on your own, we advise that you tie it to a learning management system (LMS) or have a way that you can keep checks and balances on who is viewing or attending training. You don't want your company to make an investment in your employees and "hope" that things are going as well as you'd like.

Conclusion

It is no longer a matter of if, but when your business will suffer from a cyber threat. You want your employees to be ready for anything that is thrown at them in the cyber security landscape. You know that the biggest threat to everything you have worked hard to build is your employees as the gate keepers.

Security awareness is possibly one of the simplest steps that you can take to securing your company. Investing in your team's security awareness will pay back exponentially. Cyber insurance companies will take security awareness training into consideration when they are underwriting your cyber insurance policy. A security-and-compliance-first culture in your company shows them that you are not an easy target to be picked off.

Prodigy Technology encourages all SMB companies to look into security awareness for their employees. There are various solutions and avenues that can be taken to make an impact on user education.

If you or someone in your company would like more guidance on this issue, please visit us at our website www.prodigytechnology.net and schedule a meeting with our team. If you mention this book, you will qualify for a free first two months of security awareness or a one-time 25% off any of our services.

If you would like to start a cyber security assessment of your company, please fill out the small survey at www.prodigytechnology.net/risk. We will provide all your employees with a baseline security test and dark web scan for free.

About the Author

Emilio J. Mejia is an IT & Cybersecurity professional with 17+ years of experience in the IT Field. Emilio is currently the COO & Partner at Prodigy Technology Solutions, a Managed Service Provider that helps Small & Medium businesses in South Florida & across the country manage their IT & mitigate their risk with Cybersecurity solutions.

Emilio was born in September 1986 in the Dominican Republic. His parents migrated to the US when he was only five years old. His love for computers and technology grew quickly as he began to take computers classes throughout elementary and middle school.

He applied to a vocational highschool and enrolled in the Cisco Networking Academy. Emilio went on to Graduate from DeVry University in just 3 years with his Bachelor's Degree in IT Networking & Management.

Before being approached by his partner Carlos Gomez to help him grow Prodigy Technology to the company that it is today, Emilio climbed the IT ranks from a Technician to a Senior Engineer to an IT Manager. Today Emilio and Prodigy help consult their clients through the ever-changing landscape that is IT. Prodigy focuses not only on support and professional services but on helping clients identify and mitigate their risk with cybersecurity solutions.

Prodigy Technology Solutions was awarded a position in the NextGen 101 by Channel Futures in 2021. The NextGen 101 list honors industry-leading managed services and technology providers who are driving a new wave of growth and innovation for the tech channel via the groundbreaking solutions they deliver for their customers.

What is Zero-Trust and Why Should You be Concerned as a Business Owner?

By Matt Dillon and Nick McClain

How do you protect against an attack that doesn't exist yet? On the surface, it seems like an impossible proposition: to defend your business against a cyber threat that no antivirus has ever seen before. Yet, the need for protection against these types of "zero-day" threats grow daily, as the sheer number of zero-day threats grow daily (at an ever-increasing rate). According to the United States Health and Human Services Cybersecurity Department, zero-day attacks increased 100% from 2019 to 2020. According to the *Technology Review*, this doubling of total zero-day threats year over year occurred again between 2020 and 2021. To defend against these unknown attacks, IT security firms are forced to implement new forms of defensive protocols and technologies, one of which is called zero-trust.

Created by John Kindervag in 2010, zero-trust is a framework for securing a business against emerging threats. John's motto: "never trust, always verify," speaks to the ideology behind a zero-trust framework. Now, some ten years later, John's security model is becoming increasingly popular as a response to the growing number and complexity of cyber threats. Cyber attacks were estimated to cost businesses $6 trillion dollars in 2021, which is a figure that has more than doubled in just six years. Zero-trust is not a one-license-to-purchase-and-then-done type of scenario. Rather, zero-trust is a framework or methodology for securing an organization that is comprised of multiple technologies, policies, and tools. This is an important distinction when planning a zero-trust framework. In this chapter, we will cover the different components of zero trust technology and why it is important to implement this technology in every business, regardless of employee count, revenue, or vertical.

Traditionally, cyber security focused on perimeter security. This means the focus was on "keeping out the bad" through firewalls and other defensive technology like IDS, email gateways, etc. The key flaw in this methodology is the assumption that any user or device already inside the network is safe. Zero-trust takes the opposite approach. With a zero-trust method, the network is assumed to already be compromised. Zero-trust technology is made up of multiple components, but the core idea is just as the name implies: nothing is trusted, nothing is safe. Instead of a "default allow" policy, organizations are transitioning to a zero-trust, "default deny" policy. The principles of zero-trust architecture as established by the National Institute of Standards & Technology (NIST) are:

- All data sources and computing services are considered resources.
- All communication is secure regardless of network location; network location does not imply trust.
- Access to individual enterprise resources is granted on a per-connection basis; trust in the requester is evaluated before the access is granted.
- Access to resources is determined by policy, including the observable state of user identity and the requesting system, and may include other behavioral attributes.
- The enterprise ensures all owned and associated systems are in the most secure state possible and monitors systems to ensure that they remain in the most secure state possible.
- User authentication is dynamic and strictly enforced before access is allowed; this is a constant cycle of access, scanning and assessing threats, adapting, and continually authenticating.

For a small-to-medium-sized business, implementing a zero-trust solution can be a daunting exercise. The initial implementation can be complex, and the required ongoing maintenance can be burdensome for a smaller organization to handle internally. Outsourcing to a trusted managed services provider to deploy, manage, and constantly fine-tune the zero-trust framework is recommended. The benefits, however, are more than worth the initial effort. The increased security is vital but is not always considered upfront: Implementing a zero-trust framework properly can reduce the complexity of the security system(s) and operational overhead as a whole. The number of defensive systems is reduced, as more antiquated security systems (like traditional antivirus) are deemed unnecessary in lieu of a zero-trust framework. This means fewer security programs running on each machine, which leads to an increase in performance across the board, as system resources are freed up to perform tasks not related to cyber security.

Another benefit to implementing a zero-trust framework is the ability to create a very secure BYOD (bring your own device) policy. With the proliferation of work-from-home options in today's post-COVID age, the ability to offer a BYOD policy while ensuring a high level of security is more important than ever. Zero-trust allows end users to accomplish their work roles and responsibilities without employers needing to purchase every employee a cell phone and/or a computer. Many employees prefer to utilize their own devices (especially in a remote work environment) and zero-trust gives IT professionals the ability to allow this without sacrificing security. The ability for employees to use their own devices, in conjunction with the reduction in the number of needed security applications, both equate to cost savings that can help offset the expense of the zero-trust framework itself.

Application zero-trust

When planning a zero-trust framework for an organization, there are multiple pieces of that framework to be considered. The first is application zero-trust. Traditionally, end users can install applications and updates as they please when it comes to their personal machine. The problem with this is that the end users might inadvertently (or worse, purposely) install ransomware and other forms of malware, which opens the floodgates for risk and cyber threats. With application zero-trust technology, IT admins set up a predetermined application whitelist, and ALL other applications are blocked from being installed. This ensures every single application that is installed on a company machine has been approved by an IT professional before installation. Outside of the security benefits of a setup like this, companies also benefit from increased productivity, as users are given the tools needed to accomplish their roles and are blocked from straying outside of that consistent application stack.

Network based zero-trust

The next component of a well-deployed zero trust framework is network-based zero-trust. The concept is the same: nothing is trusted unless already whitelisted. From a networking perspective, this means even devices on the internal company network cannot be explicitly trusted, which is a large departure from traditional cyber security methodologies. Traditionally, cyber security was focused on perimeter defense, meaning anything inside the perimeter (or network) was deemed "already checked" and "safe." Considering there is not a way to check for a zero-day threat, this traditional framework is becoming less and less effective as zero-day attacks are increasing daily. Since we cannot scan for a threat that has never been seen before, the cyber security industry is adopting this zero-trust method to combat the unknown threat landscape.

Application ringfencing

The third component of a well-deployed zero-trust framework is application ringfencing. This ensures threats are unable to move laterally throughout the network or company systems. Ringfencing allows a cyber security professional or team to deny one or all applications from communicating with other systems, applications, or data on the same computer or network. This ensures that any compromised system is unable to subsequently infect other systems inside the organization. This is especially beneficial when guarding against a ransomware attack, wherein the malicious application is designed to spread laterally through as much of the network as possible.

Considering the proliferation of ransomware attacks in recent years and months, ringfencing has become a necessary component of a zero-trust framework and overall cyber security plan.

Identity Management

Finally, a very important component of zero-trust is identity management, and the ability to trust adaptively.

Just because a user or device was deemed trusted an hour ago, does not automatically mean they are trusted now. This is a large departure from historical perimeter security setups where devices or users were deemed either safe or not safe, indefinitely. In a zero-trust model, trust is constantly evaluated based on several factors, including machine attributes, behavior, context, etc. The access to internal systems is adjusted in real time based on these factors (and others). The ability to trust in an adaptive way allows IT professionals to bring a new level of security, an automation to their workflow, and allows a business to ensure the highest level of security both inside and outside the perimeter network.

The United States government has recognized the need for zero-trust technology. In fact, in January 2022, the Office of Management and Budget released a memorandum requiring zero-trust architecture to be implemented federally and goes on to define specific cyber security standards that are required prior to 2024. This memorandum is in response to a growing number of attacks on our government's internal systems, which can very quickly and easily put public safety at risk. With the recent events in Ukraine and Russia, the need to secure America's internal systems has increased dramatically, and the federal government is moving quickly to defend against these new threats. Their decision to move towards a zero-trust framework solidifies the importance and necessity of implementing the same in your business. After reading this chapter, your initial thoughts might be: *I'm just a small (or medium) sized business...*

surely, I'm not a target, and these protections exceed necessity for me? This kind of technology was designed only for large corporations or government bodies! The unfortunate part of this line of thinking is that we are the new and largest targets today; low-hanging fruit tastes just as good and is easier to take. Historically, small businesses do not use the same protections a larger enterprise would, and that makes them more susceptible to risk. We need better protection(s) to meet this new reality, and zero-trust fills the security gap created by the new cyber landscape we are all living in.

Zero-trust technology is the future of cyber security. The ability to take a proactive approach to security, vs. a reactive approach, changes the game for cyber security professionals and the corporations they protect. To learn more about zero-trust technology and how it can improve and impact your business, head over to www.reciprocaltech.com.

About the Authors

Matt Dillon and Nick McClain are avid cyber security professionals with a long track record of assisting small and medium clients with fortifying their businesses against cyber threats. Together, they founded a cyber security consulting firm called Reciprocal Technologies and hold more than 25 years of cyber security and technical experience. Their partnership fuels their business, as their strengths and weaknesses play into each other's well.

Nick manages the high-level technical needs of the business, while Matt manages the client interaction and communication. Together, they manage a rapidly growing team of professionals responsible for securing thousands of endpoints.

Outside of cyber security, both Matt and Nick are car enthusiasts and enjoy attending track days, car-and-coffee events, etc.

Matt is married to his wonderful wife, Jess. Together they have two boys: Wesley, and Channing.

Nick lives the bachelor life and enjoys spending time with his (spoiled) cat, Paris and working on his personal fitness.

Here There Be Cyber Dragons

By Douglas Poirier

"Not protecting your business against cyber threats is akin to running naked through a raging forest fire while being chased by a horde of bloodthirsty Vikings."
– Unknown Hacker

Know your technology. Understand that the most common complaint about cyber security is the expense. When forced or compelled to purchase technology without fully grasping its utility and value, a business will usually respond by choosing the most cost-effective solution. Simply put, when businesses do nothing or implement substandard solutions, these offer little to no protection. This outcome is common when the owner, manager, or comptroller does not understand the technology, does not understand the threat, and does not understand the value and necessity of protection.

Would you buy a new car — a Ferrari or a Mercedes-Benz — and then put the cheapest tires on it? Would you let those tires get worn down to the belts — to the steel mesh — and still risk driving on them? Of course not. No one would — we wouldn't risk our car or our lives because we understand the consequences of bad and worn-out tires. Why would you not treat your business or organization with the same care?

There are cyber dragons out there. People, habits, threats, misinformation, and there's that which we simply do not know that puts businesses at risk. When it comes to cyber security, business owners and managers need to educate themselves on these dragons. Indeed, these dragons must be aggressively sought out and slain, lest they devour your organization.

The Dragon of Ignorance

To have a fundamental grasp on your technology is to maximize its usefulness. Do you understand what your server does? What about your firewall, antivirus, or backup? What do these technologies do and why do you need them? What's the difference between backup and disaster recovery? How much does your technology increase the productivity of your people? What is the net return on your investment in technology: do you have an idea, or do you not know? Name almost any business and they cannot operate without their technology, but few understand how reliant they are upon their technology. Now imagine that something interrupts that technology. Maybe the internet goes down. Maybe the server blows up. What would you do if your email stopped working? Each of those possibilities is a hassle, if not an outright emergency. No internet, server, email, or any of these issues can stop a business from functioning. Once you understand your technology and what it does and how it affects your profitability, you begin to understand the need for cyber security. You don't need to understand how these technologies function, but you should with absolute certainty know what they do for you and what happens when those technologies are lost and/or cease to function. What is the cost of being down for 5–7 days? Gross profit divided by 52 weeks? Do you still pay your people while you're down? How many clients would you lose? Would your reputation suffer and cause the loss of potential clients? Down time is expensive. This dragon is easy to kill: get educated!

Dragon of Cyber Crime

Know that there are people out there in the world, in your country, and in your community, that dedicate themselves with zealous fervor to breaking into your business network. They do it for the sole purpose of disrupting your business process and causing as much pain as possible. These people want your data, they want your money, or they want to sell your data to make money. And truly understanding this threat and quantifying the many ways hackers can achieve their goals, will allow you to understand and make the decision to implement a cyber security process to protect yourself.

Dragon of Denial

It will never happen to me! You think.

When I was growing up, my best friend's mom drove without car insurance for over five years. Her inspection sticker, too, was also expired for five plus years. Her explanation was that she had never been in a car accident and therefore never would be. Could there be a more toxic form of self-confirmation bias? The idea that it has never happened to you, so it could never happen to you, and therefore the possibility does not exist, is an extraordinarily dangerous belief. I hear this objection all the time when it comes to cyber security. Truth is, we have all had a virus at one time or another. But more to the point, many people who have suffered attacks don't talk about it.

Five years ago, I had my first direct experience with ransomware. The business was a break-fix client, that is to say, they only called me when something broke, and I would come in and fix it. I did not monitor their network, nor did I maintain their network. I had no contract with them despite my best efforts to convince them otherwise. This client felt they didn't need maintenance or protection; that bad stuff, it only happened to other people they didn't know. But I remember the desperate call — the owner was very discouraged. They had been struggling with ransomware for over a week. To make matters worse, the assistant's spouse, who works in the IT field, made a grievous error when he restored a backup over the existing data in an attempt to get the business up and working. Even if they wanted to pay the ransom, it was no longer an option because the encrypted data was gone. To make matters even worse, the backup had stopped working six months prior — the cloud subscription service had not expired but had run out of space, and the owner failed to notice the email alerts encouraging them to increase the business' backup storage.

One of the worst feelings I have ever experienced is telling a business owner they have lost data. It's devastating. You can see the blood drain from their face; the shock followed by denial, anger, and rationalization. The endless rationalization. I've learned over time to be as direct as possible, to not give hope. Hope prolongs the pain. The quickest and most effective way to recover from a similar circumstance, not having a backup in place, is to get things up and running again. Put together a plan, enter any data that may be recorded on paper or in memory and get back to work. Data lost is data lost forever. If this happens to you, you will never forget it.

Fortunately for my client, we were able to do something for them. We are thorough and leave no stone unturned. After searching the entire server, we found a local backup folder that was only 30 days old which had not been encrypted. The practice software provider had performed an upgrade a month earlier and backed up all the company data to this folder. Luck is a poor backup philosophy but still better than nothing. Fortunately, data loss was limited to 30 days and not six months. That's not a fun or acceptable situation and it's eminently avoidable. That organization came on as a maintenance client and has been with us ever since. Still, the dragon took a bite. Because of the initial delay in calling us, downtime was almost two weeks. Can you live with that? I don't know of any organization that would want to.

Let me tell you about one of my longest running clients. This client is in the financial services industry. Smart and successful, the owner has been with me for nearly 20 years, off and on, as a break-fix client. It's always been a painful process to convince the owner to do the right thing for the company's network and business. Always cost-conscious, always looking for the savings first, tripping over nickels to save pennies. Five years ago, I finally convinced the owner to let me monitor their network. This was not maintenance, so I provided them only with monitoring software, Windows updates, and antivirus software. It was an epic battle despite all the information I provided.

The answer was always, "It's never happened to me so I don't need it. It always happens to stupid people and I'm not stupid."

The owner is not stupid but is, in fact, an exceptionally smart individual. However, intellect is not the deciding factor. No one is immune to cyber threats, regardless of intellectual capacity. In my experience, when it comes to phishing, ransomware, malware, or viruses delivered through email or websites, it usually comes down to distraction and/or fatigue. If you're busy, really busy, or exhausted, eventually you will click on that email or click that popup from a website. And that's what happened to this client. One day, the owner opened an email, clicked on the attachment, and downloaded malware. That malware installed a virtual tunnel onto his computer and connected to remote locations unknown. We detected it and mitigated the malware before damage could be done. But if we hadn't convinced him to let us install our software on his computers, this story would have ended differently. You can be certain he would've had a disaster on his hands. Can you imagine informing clients that all their financial information—taxes, social security numbers, bank account info, portfolios, and more — had been compromised? How long would the business remain open? Would any of those clients stay with the organization? You already know the answer. The threats are real, and the consequences can be apocalyptic. The dragon almost got him, and he is now a believer. But most are not this lucky before they become believers; they must suffer days if not weeks of downtime, data loss, and the embarrassing reality of informing clients their personal data was lost or stolen. Not to mention the possibility of devastating financial consequences. Don't be that person — don't wait. Take action.

"Cyber insurance will pay for it," say some clients. This is one of my favorite objections: "Insurance will pay for it if I suffer a breach."

Are you sure? Do you know this to be an absolute truth? In May 2021, a municipality not too far from where I live experienced a cyber attack. They suffered a phishing scam and lost $1.2 million USD sent via ACH to a fraudulent account. Worse, in August of the same year, that municipality suffered a second phishing scam and sent another $1.1 million USD to hackers. Insurance paid out $600,000 USD on the first event and nothing on the second. (It is not uncommon for an organization to get hit a second time after suffering a successful cyber attack.) Insurance companies don't want to give away money. If you suffer damages, you can't expect a full pay out if you leave the keys in the ignition of your car, or the doors to your house open. You must show that you are being responsible and taking practical precautions. This is a big dragon; don't let it get you.

Dragon of Silence

Is it possible that there are people out there protecting themselves appropriately? Yes, some businesses are, but most are not. How do you know your precautions are working? Really, how do you know? There are very few organizations we audit that actually believe they are vulnerable. Backups are a good example.

Prospective clients will tell me, "Yes, we do backups every night," and they're confident.

But even if you have an IT professional and you have a disaster recovery plan, how do you know it works?

"I trust my IT professional," is what they say.

And that's good, it's great to have an IT professional you trust. It helps you sleep better at night. But when was the last time you restored a file? Sure, it's your IT professional's job to make sure things are working, but how do you know for certain?

Trust but verify. Yes, I borrowed that quote but it is prophetic.

One of our largest clients, with over $150 million USD a year in revenue, asks us to restore a file every month. We have a great disaster recovery plan for them, but every month they ask us to restore a file. At first you might think it's unnecessary. Some IT people might feel harassed, but good for my client for making sure. How else do they know things are working? Sure, you might get an email that says the backup worked correctly but how do you know the right directories are being backed up? You're not the IT professional. Backups are just one example. Be sure to talk about all your technology at least once a quarter. How are things working? Where are the reports and breakdowns? What are the new threats? Check in with your IT professional. Dragon slain.

We love to be heroes, we IT people. But in truth, it's not so much our knowledge that makes us the heroes in dire situations but the lack of knowledge on the part of our clients. When we save your bacon, we look fantastic. Clients love us. They're happy, we're happy, everyone's making money. Great! Just don't get complacent. Technology changes so quickly and it's important to stay up-to-date on the changes. New technology can mean more productivity and profitability but also more vulnerability. Just because your IT professional is godlike in your eyes does not mean you shouldn't talk to them. You won't know what your IT people are thinking and they won't know about your plans unless you communicate. A lot of potential problems can be solved simply by communicating. There is so much technology out there. Tens of thousands of applications and all kinds of hardware. Every business is its own technological ecosystem; every network its own personality. All of it is vulnerable to cyber threats. The way pieces of hardware and software interact create thousands upon thousands of potential problems; the permutations of cyber threats seem almost endless.

Slaying the Dragon

A hard truth: police cannot prevent crime, firefighters cannot prevent fires, and IT professionals cannot prevent cyber attacks. The best anyone can offer is protection, preparation, and mitigation. You can greatly reduce your profile to cyber threats by implementing the best firewalls, antivirus, antimalware, mail filters, encryption, and more. Preparation with servers, workstations, email, cloud backups, and disaster recovery make a huge impact on recovery times. If the worst happens, it is possible to recover quickly, in a day or less, provided you have the right technology implemented. To do that you'll need professionals, a crack team of cyber security experts. Cyber crime isn't going anywhere and the sooner you protect yourself, the better off you will be.

About the Author

Douglas Poirier, President & CEO, Umbral Technologies

Mentor, Cyber Security Consultant, IT Consultant, and Business Owner

Doug enjoys building teams and relationships with businesses to help them achieve success in their market space.

A member of the IT profession for over 25 years, Doug struck out on his own in 2001 and has never looked back. Next to the birth of his two beautiful and intelligent daughters, becoming a small business owner has been one of the most rewarding and fulfilling events of his life. Integrity and honesty are his core values: Tell the truth even if it hurts. His key to success is to embrace the chaos.

For recreation, Doug enjoys writing Fantasy, Horror, and Science Fiction under the non de plume D.B. Poirier.

Training Your Employees to Prevent Cyber Crime

By David Rose

Johnson and Smith had excellent cyber security tools in place. They had a next-generation firewall, advanced intrusion prevention, a SIEM, and a SOC watching over their network, but the office manager wired $275,000 USD to an account that was not recoverable. This happens far too often and is sometimes so damaging to a business that they never recover.

The problem is the people. No matter how good your security measures are, if your people continue to do the wrong things and put you at risk, it is only a matter of time before you fall victim to a breach or cyber attack with significant financial impact. Hackers know this. In a targeted attack, hackers will look for the weak link in your organization to gain a foothold. Kevin Mitnick, one of the most wanted men by the FBI for many years and world-renowned hacker, now turned cyber evangelist, gave specific examples of how he was able to access systems in a bank he was hired to penetrate using this type of social engineering and several other well-known attack methodologies. According to Mitnick, "Social engineering bypasses all technologies, including firewalls."

To solve this problem, you must train your employees and educate your team about cyber security. I enjoy talking to CEO's and business owners about deploying our phish testing and security awareness training because it is a great opportunity for management to send a clear message to the entire company:

This is important.

The risk is real.

We are taking it seriously, and actively taking steps to limit our risk.

This is what YOU can do to help protect the company and your job.

By introducing phish testing and security awareness training this way, you create a culture of cyber security. Teach employees to be skeptical about requests. Teach them to stop and ask someone before making a change, like a transfer. Teach them that if an email does not look or feel right, ask the IT team about it before proceeding. Train them. Test them. Train them when you catch them. Share results, repeat.

Do you have weekly or monthly team meetings? Do you include cyber security as part of your regular meetings? Even if you only allocate a few minutes, making cyber awareness part of your regular cadence continues to keep it top-of-mind and lets the team know how important it is.

The Process

There are many good phish testing and security awareness training products and services available on the market now. The theory of operation is consistent across most product lines: send test emails simulating phishing and spear phishing attacks to your employees. See who opens them and clicks on links, putting you at risk. Educate people that are caught to prevent them from falling victim to that type of attack again.

Depending on your management style and approach, I have seen firms roll out testing two ways. Some prefer to roll it out without notice to see who is putting them at risk in a "blind study" while others prefer to proactively let their staff know it is coming and encourage active participation by marking suspect emails as suspicious. Most phish testing software allows this option of allowing recipients to report the email as suspicious, but not all products give you that option.

Once a data sampling (typically 2-3 test emails per person) has been collected, some CEOs want the specifics of WHO we are catching, while others just want the numbers and to see that things are improving. The key is to ensure active management and action. Just as having an active alerting and action plan to deal with detections for your antivirus software is vital for protection, swiftly taking action to help your people learn to protect themselves is key to a successful program.

Being Specific

Once your baseline phish testing is complete and you have identified and educated the people with the highest risk, most products will allow you to create your own phish testing campaigns. This can be a powerful tool to train around your specific company communication and risk, as well as training the team on new attack vectors and vulnerabilities as they are discovered.

For example, if you are a law firm specializing in real estate closings, testing around email procedures and communications involving bank and wire transfers is critical. When we learn about new spear phishing attacks using the gaelic font to hide characters in website links, we can test spear phish AND train our staff to be on the lookout for this type of attack.

Additional Training and News as a Tool

New vulnerabilities and attack methods will continue to require our diligence. Sharing information in a timely manner can help reduce your risk. A few sentences repeated every month in your meetings reminding people to stop and ask IT before entering their credentials for any email is helpful. Citing specific examples in the news or from associates that fell victim to that type of attack drives the message home.

Case study

A small financial management firm had MFA activated, advanced endpoint protection with intrusion detection and intrusion prevention, but the CEO unknowingly allowed a hacker to gain access to his email account. The hacker read through many of the CEO's emails and began to email his clients, both to request payment to a fake/modified site, and to gain access to the client's confidential information. How did it happen?

The CEO was working late in the day, after having started at 7am. He had a long day. He was tired and distracted. He was on the phone, talking to his daughter about something important when an email popped up to ask him for his password. He did not think much about it, as he knew he had MFA for the account. Ten minutes later, his cell phone popped up an approval request, which he approved. He just gave the hacker full access to his account. If the hacker had sent the MFA request immediately, he probably would not have approved it. They are smart. We need to be vigilant.

In this case, the CEO called his IT company, and they quickly changed his password and verified MFA was active, and reviewed sent and received emails for appropriate action. Because he realized his mistake quickly, the impact was not too high, but he had to notify all his customers. Embarrassed, he learned an important lesson. Technology alone is not enough to keep you safe.

Conclusion

Phish testing and security awareness training are important pieces of your security stack to help you achieve cyber resilience. Continuing to train your team and speak to them regularly about cyber security helps keep security top of mind for everyone, which helps reduce your risk. Ongoing programs and industry-specific cyber training can be provided to further reduce your risk. No one can guarantee you will not be hacked or breached but you can take steps to limit your risk, and be ready when it happens so you respond properly, in a timely manner, and face the lowest possible impact from the attack.

To contact the author of this chapter or schedule a call with him, visit his company website at rosects.com. There is a link there to schedule a meeting. There is also a two-minute video about cyber security at https://rosects.com/security-first/.

About the Author

After earning his Bachelor of Arts degree from the University of Vermont in 1984, David taught himself about computers, word processing, and databases and began teaching classes in a small business in town. He went on to become a partner in that business which they grew together into a Value-Added Reseller serving Vermont businesses. In 1997, David left that business to start Rose Computer Technology Services from the basement of his home. Rose Computer Technology Services has grown and evolved over the years, pivoting numerous times as the industry has changed. Today they are a recognized leader in IT Management and Cyber Security in their marketplace. David met his wife, Cynthia while at UVM. They have been married for 33 years and have two wonderful adult children, Samuel and Isabelle. When not doing IT and Cyber Security, David enjoys skiing, golfing, martial arts, and traveling.

How to Ensure Your Remote Workers Are Not Endangering Your Business

By Brian Linning

Keeping your remote workforce from compromising your company is, in reality, extending what you should already be doing for your internal workforce and then adding layers that are unique to the needs of the mobile/remote worker.

As COVID-19 spread around the world, businesses experienced the most rapid change and adoption of remote work that has ever happened! IT professionals scrambled at a blistering pace to enable access for this remote workforce, creating new policies and procedures to safeguard their companies.

Does Your Company Have Remote Workers?

I believe that businesses fall into one of two distinct categories. The first category is companies that know and understand they have remote workers that perform a variety of tasks from wherever they are. The second is those that think that they don't have any remote workers or don't acknowledge that any work is done remotely.

Every business does some form of remote work. Email on smartphones, editing reports from a shared cloud drive, updating contact information in SalesForce, holding Zoom meetings, updating company social media: these are just a few examples of remote work being performed outside the traditional security domain of the company office. A Gallup poll in September of 2021 showed that "45% of full-time employees are working partly or fully remote."[6]

Should the Same Security Policies and Procedures be Enforced for Remote Workers as Office Workers?

We need the same or better controls for remote workers because we often don't have the same reach into the computers, smartphones, and networks they use. When workers use computers and BYOD (Bring Your Own Device) equipment in the office, we have tight control over the threat environment by creating a sterile environment for devices to connect to. We raise the shields on our firewalls, activate our weapons to destroy all malicious actions within our domain, and patch our universe with everything we can find.

According to NIST - Computer Security Division, telework and remote access solutions typically need to support several security objectives.[7] These can be accomplished through a combination of security features built into remote access solutions and the application of additional security controls to telework devices and other components of the remote access solution. The most common security objectives for telework and remote access technologies are as follows:

- Confidentiality: ensure that remote access communications and stored user data cannot be read by unauthorized parties.
- Integrity: detect any intentional or unintentional changes to remote access communications that occur in transit.
- Availability: ensure that users can access resources through remote access whenever needed.

The Cybersecurity & Infrastructure Security Agency (CISA) has guidelines for essentials in cyber security readiness. They recommend that "managing cyber risks requires building a culture of cyber readiness."[8] The essential elements of a culture of readiness are:

- Yourself (the leader of your company): Drives cybersecurity strategy, investment and culture.
- Your staff (employees): Develop security awareness and vigilance.
- Your systems (what makes you operational): Protect critical assets and applications.
- Your surroundings (the digital workplace): Ensure only those who belong on your digital workplace have access.

- Your data (what your business is built on): Make backups and avoid data loss of information critical to operations.
- Your crisis response: limit damage and quicken restoration of normal operations.

Here are nine steps for implementing NIST and CISA for protecting your company and ensuring your remote workers are not endangering your business:

1. Establishing Company Security Policies

Well-run companies have employee handbooks which clearly define company human resource policies such as:

- Employment Basics
- Workplace Polices
- Code of Conduct
- Compensation & Professional Development
- Benefits and Perks
- Working Hours, Paid Time Off, and Vacation
- Employee Resignation & Termination

These same companies need policies that cover information technology. Written policies avoid ambiguity and allow employees to act with confidence and empowerment when a situation arises.

The following IT policies are as critical as a well-crafted human resources policy.

Information Security Policy – Defines the areas of Personally Identifiable Information (PII), protection against unauthorized access to sensitive information, and defines reasonable protection for anticipated threats. Designating a security officer for the company to implement, design, oversee, and maintain the information security policy is critical. This role could be assigned to an internal employee or third party that works closely with an internal employee. For small businesses, this role is often filled by a vCIO (virtual chief information officer) or trusted security consultant with the knowledge and expertise to define policies.

Termination Policy – Defines the processes that must occur when an employee changes positions within a company or leaves the company altogether. Removing an employee's virtual and physical access to systems should be detailed to ensure all access has been revoked. History has shown us that threat actors often use credentials from terminated employees to gain access to company systems.

Incident Response Policy – Defines what actions to take when a breach occurs. Identifying the breach or threat, what systems have been affected, what actions are necessary to document the incident, stopping further access, restoring systems, and notification of effected parties should be defined in this policy.

Network Security Policy – Defines the protections put in place for anything attached to company systems. This covers servers, desktops, software, SaaS (Software as a Service), physical networks, and wireless networks. Securing PII and IP (Intellectual Property) starts at physical access points and extends into non-physical points.

Computer Use Policy – Defines the general understanding of what is acceptable use for company equipment and systems. Defines whether personal use of company assets is allowed and clearly states that personal use will be monitored/controlled to protect company systems, along with any other general use cases.

BYOD (Bring Your Own Device) Policy – This policy clearly defines what happens when an employee uses a personal device (computer, smartphone, tablet, etc.) for company use. This use may be to access the office network or remotely access the company network/ systems. Deployment of company security solutions to a BYOD device would be defined in this policy.

Sanction Policy – Outlines the actions to take should an employee violate any of the IT policies.

Equipment and Data Disposal Policy – Details how physical equipment is decommissioned. How to securely destroy data from internal systems and software as well as SaaS services.

Facility Access & Security Policy – Defines who has physical access to secure systems, when they are allowed to access them, and how they access them. This policy should also detail environmental threats like fire, weather (tornados, hurricanes, etc.), building break-ins, and vandalism.

2. Providing Secure Connectivity

Your company's remote workforce needs reliable and secure connectivity to company systems and services. WiFi connectivity options abound and perennial favorites like coffee shops, hotels, airports, convention centers, and libraries, all offer free, unsecure WiFi access. Using these options poses one of the highest security risks for remote working.

Creating a private company VPN (Virtual Private Network) will create the shield needed in your battle to protect your data, systems, and company from unforeseen threats.

Public VPN services do not provide security for company data. Their purpose is mainly to allow anonymous access to internet services. Often, users are blocked from sites restricted by location or for other reasons and a public VPN can allow someone to subvert these restrictions.

3. Securing Access via Passwords and Multifactor Authentication

Password access to computer systems and services has been a mainstay for decades. Little has changed with them other than the need for greater complexity to avoid brute force attacks. But threat actors seldom use brute force attacks these days due to the time it takes to crack passwords this way. They've switched to phishing, vishing, smishing, and searching the dark web for this type of data.

But protecting user passwords is still a critical step. It's vital to use a secure password manager that can assist users in creating a complex random password for each individual service and then securely store those credentials.

Enabling multi-factor authentication or two-factor authentication (MFA/2FA) further enhances a security posture for systems and data protection. MFA/2FA either adds a second layer of protection after a password is entered or replaces the password altogether. They can be implemented in many ways: MFA applications, text messages, emails to a known/secure email account, etc. Password management applications often integrate this into their platforms as well.

4. Protecting systems with EDR, XDR, Zero Trust, and more

Viruses, malware, ransomware, phishing, vishing, smishing, OH MY! Stopping these threat vectors requires not one tool, but a carefully chosen set of comprehensive and complementary services and tools. Some of the ways these threats can infiltrate systems are:

- Browsing websites
- Email
- Direct messaging applications (Slack, Discord, Signal, etc.)
- Video meeting software (Zoom, Microsoft Teams, Google Meets, etc.)
- Social media (Facebook, Twitter, LinkedIn, Instagram, etc.)
- Unknown/suspicious applications
- "Free" software
- Remote access solutions
- Cloud storage services

The tools and services we use to protect systems should include, but are not limited to:

- DNS filtering
- Email filter & security
- Endpoint detection and response (EDR)

- eXtended detection and response (XDR)
- Zero-trust application & storage whitelisting
- SaaS monitoring and protection

5. Installing Firewalls

Hardware and software firewall solutions have been a staple in network security for years. Firewalls not only protect internal networks from direct connections to the internet, but they also act as secure pipelines for remote workers by creating VPNs.

Business class firewall solutions are very different from the firewall solutions that home users typically have. Business class solutions employ:

- Deep packet inspection
- Intrusion prevention services (IPS)
- SSL/TLS decryption and inspection
- Rules-based connection filtering
- Failover connectivity/SD-WAN

Some EDR and XDR solutions include firewall or firewall-like services as part of their solutions for mobile end-points. This allows remote users to have protection wherever and whenever they connect.

6. Managing Device Changes and Updates

Every device an employee uses will eventually need to have changes to security policies and software/system patches applied. Managing these across disparate platforms and operating systems can be a daunting task. But solutions do exist to ease the burden of installation/deployment of updates and provide health monitoring of managed systems.

Hardware and software inventories can be an additional benefit to a device management solution. This data can be used to create budgets for hardware replacement, software licensing, planned upgrades, and check resource utilization.

Management solutions should also include an option for remote device deactivation and wiping of all data. A stolen or lost device, even with data encryption enabled, can still be considered a risk to company security.

7. Training and Testing

Training and testing are often overlooked as a safeguard to keeping your business safe. Providing end user training around what a phishing email looks like, what an illicit text message looks like, how to spot a dangerous website, or what a suspicious voicemail sounds like is critical.

Ongoing training with follow-up testing ensures employees are kept up-to-date on the latest tactics hackers are using to "gain your employee's confidence." We have all heard the stories about the accounting department receiving an email from the CEO, directing them to wire money to an offshore account. Training and policies help craft a defense against this form of deception and theft.

8. Encrypting Data

Your company data is the gold at the end of a hacker's rainbow. Once they've gotten past your passwords, MFA/2FA, bypassed your VPNs, breached your firewall, suppressed your EDR tools and/or stolen your equipment (laptop, smartphone, desktop, server, etc.) they now want that payday. Your last defense is encryption! Making your data unusable if they get that far will keep your data safe.

Data encryption use to be a difficult or awkward process for end users. Separate software, passwords, and procedures made daily routine access to information difficult, and impacted worker productivity. Today, there are many ways that make data encryption and daily access easy for every user. Tools like BitLocker for Windows, FileVault for Mac OS, and other data-at-rest encryption tools make the process easy for end users to access data-at-rest on their devices (data housed physically on computer data storage in a digital form) while keeping it all secure and safe.

9. Safeguarding Data Everywhere

While critical data should reside on company servers or in cloud data vaults, oftentimes important information is located on local or remote user's systems. Backing up this data as well as their entire system is vital to a complete data security plan. End user device backups will allow for quick restoration of not only individual files, but also allow for quick recovery should a system fail or get stolen.

What Can You Do To Protect Your Business and Implement These Steps?

Do it yourself - DIY would include but is not limited to:

- Creation of:
    - Overall guidelines
    - Policies
    - Standard operating procedures (SOP)
- Acquisition of security solutions
    - Software
    - Services
- Hiring a security professional to work inhouse
- Staffing a help desk for day-to-day support
- Continuous training of IT staff

Plan for significant budgetary expenses to make all this happen. You also should consider that your company isn't a security solutions and systems integrations company. Doing this will distract you from doing what you and your company do best.

Hire a security solutions and systems integration company - This option will lower your overall cost, provide highly-skilled experts, streamline the overall process, and deliver a complete customized solution based on the size and industry of your business.

Linning Associates has the expertise, knowledge, processes, tools, and people to work with your business to execute these nine steps, and more. Our clients consider us trusted partners that help handle all the tech stuff so they can focus on their business.

About the Author

Brian Linning is the Founder and CEO of Linning Associates based in Northern Illinois. Linning Associates is an established security technology consulting and systems integration firm providing business improvement solutions. Brian holds the firm belief that CEOs and business owners should spend their time and focus on growing their business and not on their technology.

Brian has over 30 years of professional experience. Brian has worked with a Fortune 100 company as well as consulting with a wide variety of local Small Businesses including the Food Industry, Construction, Pet Care, Medical, Legal, Insurance, Printing & Packaging, and more.

Brian has been a speaker at local and national events on topics such as IT security, Implementing Voice over IP systems, Line of Business Applications – Which One & Why, The Importance of Prioritizing IT Costs, and other IT related topics.

Contact Brian to discuss how Linning Associates can be your trusted partner to protect your business from cybersecurity threats while streamlining your business systems.

LetsChat@Linning.Associates
847-416-6770
www.Linning.Associates

Are SMBs At Risk of a Cyber Attack -- What is the Likelihood That My Business Will Be Hacked?

By Alan Stukenholtz

Dean has a small T-shirt company. Like many small business owners, Dean wants to make as much money as he can and doesn't have a large budget for IT. Oftentimes, clients will ask Dean to come up with new logos or ask him to match existing artwork or logos so he can print whatever they might need. The fonts that are needed are often not available to Dean from his computer, so he will search the internet looking for the correct fonts. Dean could pay a subscription fee to a popular site that has all the fonts he would ever need, but he doesn't want to spend the extra money, so he usually searches for free fonts he can use. Sometimes the sites he gets his fonts from are a little bit questionable, but it's ok — when Dean is working on artwork, it's usually late at night when no one else is around.

Dean is mainly a graphic artist, but he's also the book-keeper, marketing director, and salesperson. Plus, he spends a lot of time in the workshop working on products. He's been in business for about five years now and has worked up quite a large book of clientele. A year ago, he expanded his business so that he could do promotional items — like pens and water bottles — and he also has a small embroidery machine, although most of that work he sends off to a third party.

For a lot of the small businesses Dean works for, he is the sole creator of their designs. He keeps all of his artwork on his computer, and a local PC repair company helped him set up an external hard drive on his machine that he can back up to every night. They also helped him get set up on his email, one that he gets free from his internet service provider, and they set him up with a free antivirus program to help keep his computer safe from viruses.

Quite a lot of businesses are set up this way. Back in 1997, when I started my first computer company, we were installing Windows 95, and didn't really bother that much with antivirus or security. It was pretty hard for a hacker to gain access to your system because you had to create a dial-up connection to the internet and you weren't on for very long because you didn't want to tie up the phone lines. People weren't thinking that much about getting hacked, not even the government. But in February 2001, a guy named Gary McKinnon hacked into 97 different NASA computers and the United States military. McKinnon was able to log in, look at files, and manipulate them or delete them if he wanted. And this was all with a dial-up modem. McKinnon's hack was mostly recreational, he wasn't trying to get money, or shut down the government, but it was a wake-up call for the United States government.

WAIT! I'm not the government, no one wants what I have

Dean is not the US government either; he doesn't have top secret files sitting on a server somewhere. He's just a small business owner. His company revenue is less than $200,000 a year. He's not worried about being hacked. He's a small company, and no one really wants what he has. If something did happen to his computer, he has the backup that his computer company helped him set up.

Everyone assumes they are ok if they have a backup

One evening, Dean was up late working on a new graphic for one of the local youth soccer teams. It had been a long day and after he left, a bat had flown in from outside, setting off his office's alarm system around 4am. So he had to go in early and meet the police at his office. He didn't think he could go back to sleep, so he just stayed and started working on some of his customer orders. One of his employees called in sick, so he had to cover for all the work that he had set up for his employee to do that day. It was 9pm, and Dean was still at work.

Captain, we can't get the shields up, the ship is just too tired

Dean was almost done with this very long day but decided to check email before he left just to make sure he had covered everything he needed for the next day. One of his new emails was from his ISP.

Dean,

Your email account may have been compromised, please log in to your account using the link below and reset your password.

Your Internet Service Provider.

This was just a perfect end to a perfect day. Dean clicked the link, and a website came up that asked him for his current password and a new password. Dean grabbed his password sheet out of the top drawer of his desk and located his email password. He typed in his old password and completed the form to create a new one. After scratching out his old email password on his sheet and writing down the new one, he stuck his password sheet back into his desk, locked up the office, and went home.

Not All Hacks are Obvious

The next couple of months for Dean were uneventful. Everything was going pretty well for Dean. Business was great, he had gained a couple of good-sized contracts for promotional items, and he was thinking about hiring another person because it was getting hard to fulfill all the orders coming in. Dean had taken out a line of credit with his bank for $25,000: the third-party company that produced his promotional items required payment for orders up-front, and Dean didn't want to have to ask his customers to pay him for products before they received them. His bank set him up with a line of credit so he could place the orders and get the money from the customers later. His bank had helped him set up online banking so he could easily transfer money from his line to his account.

Dean's week was going pretty well, he had gotten all of his orders turned in for the week, and he had a big fishing trip planned with some friends for the weekend, so he closed down right at five o'clock on Friday and headed off with his friends.

Monday morning, Dean showed up for work around 7am; he was feeling well-rested from his fishing trip. It was a normal morning. He got into the office, started the coffee pot, and sat down at his computer to start the new week. He had a change that he needed to make on a graphic for some T-shirts they were starting on that week, so he got onto his computer and proceeded to open the file he needed to work on when he got this error:

"The file is corrupt and cannot be opened."

Dean tried to open a few more files and got the same error. Dean wasn't sure what to do; he could find his way around a computer, but he only knew what was related to his work. Dean looked on his computer for his backup program. He knew the PC repair company had put backup software on his computer a couple of years ago, but he couldn't remember what it was called. He'd have to wait for the PC repair company to open at 9am — he'd just call and get the name of the software they put on his computer and everything would be fine.

As soon as the clock hit 9am, Dean picked up the phone and called his repair company. They couldn't remember what software they put on his computer. They named a few, but Dean couldn't find any of them. They told him they would send someone to take a look at his computer.

They told Dean he'd been hacked and they probably still had access, so he should just shut down his computer and wait for them. It took them a few hours to get onsite and Dean really needed his computer before too long or he was going to be dead in the water. When the technician arrived, he immediately noticed what was gong on. The tech told Dean that it looked like he had been hacked, and that all his files were encrypted. There was a notepad file in every directory that explained how Dean could get his files decrypted. He also couldn't find any software that could be used for a backup, and there were no files on the external hard drive. Dean allowed the PC repair company to take his computer to see if they could get anything back. Maybe tomorrow would be a better day.

Dean checked with the PC repair company the next day, and they still had not found a solution. They told Dean he could pay the ransom, but it was going to cost him about $10,000. *I have a line of credit*, he thought, *maybe I'll just use that to get my files back*. Dean called the bank that afternoon, he still wasn't sure if he wanted to pay the ransom to get his files back but he had years of work on his hard drive, a lot of work that he just couldn't reproduce without a lot of work. He told his banker he couldn't access his online banking because his computer was in for repairs, and he needed to transfer some money from his line of credit account.

His banker said, "Dean, I'm sorry the maximum amount has already been used from your line of credit."

This didn't seem right; he had only established the line of credit earlier that month. The bank proceeded to tell him that his online bill payments were used to write a check, which was then sent to a PO box in California. And the check had already cleared. Dean's bank account was almost dry. Someone took everything in his line of credit and left $500 in his bank account.

What If a Hacker Took Everything in *Your* Bank Account?

Do you remember a few months back when Dean got that email from his ISP about changing his password? That was the work of hackers. Dean didn't really have a problem with his account, and his password was never changed. The hackers were able to convince Dean that his account needed a new password — Dean was tired, and didn't think the entire situation through. When Dean entered his old password, the hackers were able to gain access to his email account. His real account was never changed, and since Dean had all his passwords saved in his email program, he never knew any different. Dean also had an outdated, free antivirus software that didn't protect him against bad websites. When he loaded the fake website and completed all the information, the website loaded a trojan horse on his computer, which **gave the hackers full remote access to his computer**.

I'd like to point out that the actual event didn't happen until the **hackers had been on his computer for months**. Let's repeat that so it can sink in:

HACKERS HAD BEEN ON HIS COMPUTER FOR MONTHS.

Dean was running a very successful business, and was an expert in his field, however, Dean didn't know the risk he was taking. He thought his backups were good, his email acceptable, and his computer security was good enough.

As a business owner, you can easily convince yourself that hackers don't want what you have. Your business is just too small and too insignificant to be a target of hackers. The truth is, many hackers do a forensic analysis of your computers and servers. Lots of times, they find avenues to revenue that you don't anticipate. Your files might not be important, but what about your bank account? What about the customers that you communicate with? Have you opened the door for a hacker to target them as well?

It's Easier to Break into a Car Than Fort Knox

Hackers don't care about the size of your business. SMBs are targets because it's easier to break down their security. Sure, big companies like Berkshire Hathaway and Volkswagen are large targets, and probably receive thousands of hacking attempts every minute, but as the size and wallet gets larger, so does their IT budget and security. Most SMBs don't have a large IT budget, and security is low. This makes SMBs a prime target.

It was the PC Repairman's Fault, Right?

Typical computer repair shops fix problems as they come in. The client calls because of a problem, then the problem is fixed. It is a reactive approach. Often, they don't have the knowledge or resources to do more for you. They aren't responsible for day-to-day management of your network and systems. But managed services providers offer ongoing support that uses a more proactive approach. Things like patches, security, and backups are all monitored.

Now think about Jane, who is the receptionist for a small accounting firm. Their PC repair company charges $200/hr. When Jane has a problem, her boss wants her to do everything she can to fix it herself, so they don't have to incur a large service bill. These types of scenarios are common with SMBs. If Jane gets a suspicious email or popup on her computer, she's probably not going to call for help, but could very possibly make a disastrous decision.

Start a Conversation About Cyber Security

Your service company may have services that cover cyber security, or they may not. Your best bet as an SMB is to have a conversation with your IT provider and see what they offer. If you are on a service plan now, you need to call and make sure that your plan is comprehensive enough to cover cyber security.

Ask your insurance agent for cyber liability insurance. Often, the questionnaire that an agent will have you fill out will expose shortcomings in your current service offering. Your IT provider should also be able to do an insurance evaluation.

Simple Managed Services are Not Enough

Cyber crime has become more sophisticated over the years. Simple antivirus and patching is not enough. You need a comprehensive plan that only a service provider that focuses on cyber security can provide. At Starr Computer Solutions, Inc., our focus is on cyber security, and we would love to provide you with a comprehensive plan and ongoing support. Call or email us today to get started.

Starr Computer Solutions, Inc.

620-225-1499

www.starrtech.net

About the Author

Alan Stukenholtz is President, CEO, and founder of Starr Computer Solutions, Inc. established in 1997. He discovered his love for computers while studying at Kansas University and decided to leave school and go back home to Dodge City, Kansas and work for a small computer company. Shortly thereafter, Alan and a few colleagues started Starr Computer Solutions with funding from another local business. In 1999, the company started operating a Dial-up Internet service, which soon became a DSL provider, and then a wireless Internet service provider.

In 2003 after his previous colleagues had left the business, he purchased the company and took over as President, scaling down and working from his home office. He purchased a security company shortly after and got into the business of security and camera systems, continuing with IT.

Alan is a father of two, and a husband to his wonderful wife Carla. He coaches youth ice hockey and plays in an adult league. He loves to play the guitar, sing, and play tuba in the local community band.

Alan's experience in IT since 1995 has made him an expert in the field of IT and cyber security, gaining knowledge from his experience and any good information he can get his hands on. Alan believes that you can never know it all, and that you have to constantly learn and grow to stay on top.

Alan Stukenholtz
CEO/President
Starr Computer Solutions, Inc.
astuke@starrtech.net
620.225.1499

Cloud Security: Creating A More Effective Method for Safeguarding Data

By Ryan O'Hara

"All of our information is in the cloud, so our business is secure." This is one of the most common responses I hear when I ask business owners about their cyber security.

Unfortunately, those business owners are wrong. Here's why.

The "cloud" refers to basically any system or service that runs on a remote machine over the internet. Cloud services include everything from a virtual machine running in a data center to a web service or application accessed via a browser. Some common examples would be Microsoft 365, Google Workspace and QuickBooks Online. Cloud services have allowed businesses to scale faster and more affordably than ever before, while maintaining a consistent, predictable budget.

While cloud services can be set up securely — and in my opinion, can be even more secure than traditional on-premises operations — they are typically not secure "out of the box."

Security Risks in the Cloud

Most cloud providers, as the vendors selling a product, are primarily concerned with making the sale and ensuring a positive user experience afterwards. They try to make the product as easy to set up and use as possible, and this often comes at the expense of basic security.

First, let's tackle one major assumption: many businesses believe that, since the information is on the cloud provider's platform, the provider is liable or responsible for security. In most cases, this could not be further from the truth.

When you first sign up for a cloud service, you must agree to their terms of service. Most people never read these and simply assume that the vendor is taking responsibility. In reality, these terms of service tend to clearly spell out that the cloud provider is *not* liable or responsible for any loss of data due to things like compromise, disaster, accidental deletion, or pretty much any other reason your data could be impacted.

In fact, most vendors recommend investing in additional third-party backups to protect your data. With the exception of some sort of gross negligence on the part of the vendor, all liability and responsibility is on you.

One of the biggest advantages to having information in the cloud is the ability to access it from anywhere. When information was stored locally at an office, you had to be on the same network or using virtual private network (VPN) clients. When your data is in the cloud, all you need is an internet connection. The flip side of this, however, is that the same thing is true for an attacker, especially with cloud solutions right out of the box. Bad actors can connect to and attempt to access your information the same way you can. If they are able to guess or obtain your username and password (and if you don't have MFA enabled—more on that below) then the attacker can acquire the same level of access as you.

Fortunately, you're about to learn six key ways to lock your data down to block access from unauthorized parties and prevent them from accessing your information.

Increasing Security in the Cloud

Many cloud solutions come with security features — but it's usually on you as the business owner to enable them. One major security feature often left disabled by default is multi-factor authentication (MFA). This feature tends to be turned off to streamline the user experience.

MFA adds a secondary layer to the login process, requiring you to enter a code texted to your phone or from an app in addition to your username and password. This feature provides considerable bang for the buck when securing access to your cloud services. While user experience is important, the damage that can occur as a result of not using MFA far outweighs the minor inconvenience of adding another step to logging on.

Another method of securing your information is using geographic restrictions. Typically, a business's staff operates from a single location or a small handful of predictable locations. For example, if your business is in the United States, then most of your staff will log in from the US. Thus, log in attempts from outside the US are likely unauthorized and possibly malicious.

Geographic restrictions make it possible to only allow logins from the US and block attempts from other countries, which considerably limits the footprint from which a bad actor can launch an attack. In the event that you have remote users in other locations, or someone needs to access information while travelling, you can add exceptions.

A third method of increasing security involves the use of known devices. In this case, a user can only connect from devices known to the system that have been specifically permitted to access the information. This not only helps prevent access by unauthorized parties, but can also help ensure that only devices with approved security methods can touch your information. This is especially beneficial since a user's home computer, which lacks your company's security software, could have a virus that winds up being just as disastrous as a hacker.

In addition to restricting access to known or managed devices, you can enforce compliance requirements for those devices. Your business probably already has security standards for each machine, such as an antivirus or endpoint detection and response (EDR) software and device encryption to keep the machine protected.

What if someone manages to disable those features, or a failure occurs, leaving that machine vulnerable? That puts any information the machine interacts with at risk. Robust compliance policies can monitor devices and ensure that relevant security features exist and are active before allowing the device to connect to your cloud services and systems.

Depending on the nature of your data, you can take yet another step to increase security. If you are dealing with highly sensitive information, you can implement features that lock down access to specific points of origin, such as IP addresses. For example, if you know a user will always connect to your cloud service from a specific, unchanging IP address (like an office or secure network), you can restrict access to that address. Anyone who tries to connect from anywhere else will be blocked.

Finally, cloud-based firewall systems are becoming more popular. Cloud-based firewalls allow businesses to integrate an even higher level of restriction. These systems operate just like traditional high-end, unified threat management (UTM) hardware-based firewalls. However, because they are cloud-based, they follow a device wherever it connects to the internet.

These cloud-based firewalls have a software agent that facilitates a secure connection to the firewall, which means all traffic in and out of the device is filtered, scanned, and monitored — just as if they were physically in an office and connected to the company network. Since all traffic goes through the firewall, you can also incorporate the IP address restrictions discussed above, allowing you to lock down access to a single network.

Key Takeaways

Cloud-based systems and services have been a game changer for businesses, and the days of onsite servers and application hosting are quickly disappearing. The past several years have also seen an exponential rise in cyber attacks. It's become more and more important to ensure that new technologies are properly secured and monitored.

Even the most robust and restrictive system is not totally immune to compromise. Monitoring for signs of compromise is just as important as trying to prevent it in the first place. It's critical to have systems to monitor access and activity within your cloud services. For example:

- Are attackers continually attempting to log in to a particular account?
- Did a user log in from multiple locations a great distance away in a short period of time?
- Is an account downloading or modifying an unusual number of files in a short period of time?

All of these could be signs that a compromise has occurred. Identifying an attack early can mean the difference between a minor inconvenience and a company-wide event resulting in considerable downtime, lost revenue, and fines or legal restitution.

As the business owner, it's *your* responsibility — *not* the cloud provider's — to ensure your information is protected wherever it lives. You can't assume cloud services are secure out of the box just because you are paying a provider. In fact, I can pretty much guarantee they are not.

I understand that security can be complicated, confusing, expensive, and inconvenient, but trust me: the alternative is considerably worse. If you decide to go it alone and only take one lesson from this chapter, make sure you enable MFA on *everything*. If you're using an application or service that doesn't offer MFA, find a different option. If everyone adopted MFA, the amount of cyber crime would drop overnight.

However, one of the best investments you can make for your business is to find a trusted IT provider who understands and focuses on security. Given today's cyber threats, a trusted cyber security partner is just as important as a good attorney, CPA, or insurance agent.

If you liked this chapter and would like to know more about cyber security and how you can protect your business, Ryan and his company Sphinx Cybersecurity operate a free Facebook group called "Cybersecurity Secrets for Professional Service Firms." Use the link below to find out more and join the group:

https://group.sphinxcyber.com

About the Author

Ryan O'Hara is an entrepreneur, cybersecurity expert and founder of Sphinx Cybersecurity, an IT and Cybersecurity service provider in Dearborn, MI.

Ryan founded Sphinx in 2009, after working for several years in corporate IT, to bring enterprise-level IT to small and medium-sized businesses. Sphinx has grown from its early service and support roots to become a security first managed service provider (MSP), specializing in keeping businesses throughout the United States secure and ready to handle today's rapidly evolving world of cybersecurity.

Ryan can be reached as follows:

Sphinx Cybersecurity
Phone: (313) 482-9930
Email: ryan@sphinxcyber.com
Website: https://sphinxcybersecurity.com

The Economic Impact of a Cyber Attack

by Tom McIntyre

One day, Diane gets an email from Phil in a reply to one of the batch request email messages she sent. There were recently some changes in the business and a large number of one-time payments were being requested by Phil for Diane to set up. This particular email was a request by Phil to Diane to send $300,000 by wire transfer to a specific bank account. The email was legit looking, and it wasn't unusual for this to happen. It even came from Phil using the email account of one of his other businesses. It was his normal method of communicating. He was requesting the payment be set up right away. It was time sensitive and had to be done by the end of the day. Diane communicated back and forth with Phil. The request was also sent to Randy for the required second signature. But Diane wasn't emailing with the real Phil, and the fake Phil was insistent that Diane send it immediately. Of course, Diane pushed back. They needed two signors to authorize, and she wasn't one of them. Fake Phil persisted. He suggested they talk after the weekend. Diane, in frustration, stopped communicating with fake Phil because he didn't seem to be getting it.

She said, "My part is done."

She told Phil, "You and Randy need to authorize the payment."

Over the weekend, the transfer expired. Here is where the security policy with the bank comes into play. Remember, we said two parties needed to authorize bank transfers. Diane wasn't one of the parties authorizing. Real Phil and Randy had to process the payment. Since fake Phil was unable to convince Diane or Randy, the money wasn't transferred.

On Monday, real Phil called Diane to tell her his email had been compromised. This explained the event on Friday. The criminal was able to study and learn about the organization and was somewhat familiar with their internal processes. This allowed him to proceed with the scam. We suggested to our client, the controller, that they put a process in place in addition to the bank security. When a nonstandard request is made, have a verbal approval as a backup. Normal day-to-day methods can continue as always. The potential loss to the organization was $300,000. Luckily, they were saved from that scam!

This incident was done through an email account being compromised. The criminal was impersonating one of the people in the organization. In another incident, the City of Burlington in Ontario, Canada was caught up in a similar scam. The city officials revealed that they were victims of a sophisticated email scam. In this incident, an obviously high-level city official wired $503,000 CAD (approximately $375,000 USD), to a bank account owned by the scammer. From reports of the incident, the criminal used email to have the payment of bills from a regular supplier to the City of Burlington go to a new bank account. With no obvious process in place, the money was sent by wire — no questions asked. Nobody felt the need to question the change of accounts. There should have been a process in place to confirm the changes. The City of Burlington has said they have taken necessary steps to prevent this from happening in the future. This shows the importance of training staff and having very well-defined policies and procedures in place.

The potential loss in these examples was about $675,000 US. It demonstrates that both government and small businesses are potential targets. There is no place for complacency. It's not relevant whether you are a government institution or a small business that gets scammed out of $5000. Diligence is equally important. These two examples of fraud used email impersonation to take businesses' hard earned cash. There are many other ways to accomplish this. Some involve other methods of attack that don't necessarily use email. They all demonstrate the need for strong policies and procedures that are followed and occasionally reviewed.

Ransomware has disrupted everything from food and fuel supply to health care. Federal governments have even been compromised. It not only costs cash but has a huge impact on all areas of business including downtime, reputation, and the actual ransom payments. Although the loss of cash is most recognized, it may not be the largest loss. Depending on the amounts and the demands of insurance companies or regulatory compliance, the forensics and recovery costs can add significant strain on a business when trying to recover. These costs can be both time and cash. What if the data is lost or unrecoverable, what are the costs? Every business or institution has varying numbers. If data is leaked, then there are legal ramifications and defending your reputation adds to the loss. Tech time to repair the network and rebuild the data sources can be significant not only in logistical costs but in actual lost hours of production.

The following information is from the IBM Security report, "Cost of a Data Breach Report 2021" (costs are in USD).

The increase in average total cost of a breach, 2020-2021 is 10%:

> "Data breach costs rose from $3.86 million to $4.24 million, the highest average total cost in the history of this report. Costs were significantly lower for some of organizations with a more mature security posture, and higher for organizations that lagged in areas such as security AI and automation, zero trust, and cloud security."

The lost business share of total breach costs is 38%:

> Lost business represented 38% of the overall average and increased slightly from $1.52 million in the 2020 study. Lost business costs included increased customer turnover, lost revenue due to system downtime and the increasing cost of acquiring new business due to diminished reputation.

This one is huge. The per record cost of personally identifiable information is $180. Personally identifiable information known as PII is information such as a driver's license, health cards, credit cards and social security cards. It was the most common type of record lost and was included in 44% of breaches:

When you look at the loss of data more closely you can see that the costliest type of record stolen was PII. Costs average about $180 per record. The average cost per record went up in 2021 by $146 per lost or stolen record over the 2020 amount.

Organizations with better security protections and automated processes experienced 80% lower breach costs that those organizations without those protections. This clearly indicates companies with better cyber crime awareness were in a better position to protect themselves. They were also associated with a faster time to identify and contain the breach.

There are different types of attacks on data. Ransomware and a data breach to name a couple have similar costs. The cost similarities in the attacks include lost business, recovery escalation, lost business and response costs are but a few. The cost of a Ransomware attack can escalate significantly if the ransom is paid. Breach attacks in some instances also include Ransomware.

When you look at the numbers as a small business owner, it looks formidable, and the first thought in your mind is, *That could never happen to me. Look how big those numbers are!* Keeping in mind those are averages — some of those upper numbers are in the tens of millions of dollars. It's not unusual for a small business to have 10,000 or more records on their servers. Using the figure of $180 per record, the average cost for a small business with just 10,000 records would be $1.8 million. Those numbers may seem high to the average small business owner. Every business is different. Consider the cost of the PII lost mentioned earlier. The reputation costs and regulatory compliance fines add up quickly. Insurance often is not going to cover those costs if the policies and procedures identified in the application are not followed.

In conclusion, data loss can be as little as the time to rewrite a single document to millions of dollars paid out in ransom. As a business, the important thing to understand is that there is a cost. Your risk tolerance will determine your actions. How much data can you afford to lose? How long can you afford to be without that data? How much are you willing or able to pay in the event you lose some or all of your information? Every business has a different risk tolerance. The more sensitive you are to that risk, the more value can be placed on your data.

Many businesses go under after a catastrophic failure. How do you want to manage your risk?

At **TAG Computer Services, our clients trust we understand their business**. Our clients offer professional services and have set criteria for their offices. We take the time to learn their businesses to fully understand what is required for their IT network. Working with legal firms, real estate brokerages, and dental offices, we understand how one blip in the system can affect the functionality of your team and **the security of their data.**

For more information, visit our website at https://www.yourtech.ca.

About the Author

At an early age, Tom McIntyre dreamed of being the President of a Company. In 1994 that dream came true when he started TAG Computer Services, an IT and Managed Service provider in the Niagara Region of Ontario Canada.

TAG was formed to simplify IT and help small to medium-sized businesses use technology to support growth. In more recent times, Cyber Security has been the prime focus in protecting business data. Tom has positioned the company to be a valuable resource in protecting data from vulnerabilities both inside and outside the organization.

Tom can be reached as follows:

TAG Computer Services

Phone: 905 892 4000

Email: info@yourtech.ca

Website: https://yourtech.ca

How Business Owners Can Protect Their Data from Hackers

By Mitch Redekopp

In recent years, we have been seeing a huge uptick in cyber attacks, which has forced us to pivot our business from solely "your IT provider" to "your IT provider, your cybersecurity professional, your cyber insurance policy compliance officer, and more." Without proper systems and training in place, your data is at risk.

Take, for example, eight months ago, when the accountant for a small business in our city sent us an email — subject line: Emergency!!! Please help! After skimming the body, I picked up the phone and gave them a call. They explained that they had received an email from an employee, telling them that the employee had recently changed their banking information, a mere day before payroll was to be processed. The accountant had not thought anything of it as the name on the email was the usual, and went ahead and made the bank deposit information change. On payroll day, the employee reached out to the accountant wondering where their pay was! The accountant asked about the bank information change, which the employee had no clue about. The accountant was a victim of a spoofing attack.

What happened was that a cyber criminal had spoofed the employee's first and last name and knew that the accountant was in charge of payroll, emailing them to ask for the bank info change. The accountant was not trained to look out for emails like this and didn't even look past the name before processing the change. A simple banner every time an email came from an external sender would have stopped this attack, but there was no IT company helping them because, "No hacker would ever target us," the owner would say.

When we investigated further, the email was just a simple bunch of scrambled letters @gmail.com with the employee's first and last name plastered on top. They called the bank and were able to get the funds back, but, boy, was that a scare and a wake-up call. The company now has the training and processes in place to ensure this doesn't happen again.

When we think about hackers, most still picture the nerdy adult in a dark hoodie, living in their parents' basement, cans of energy drinks lining their computer desk. The truth?

Criminal hackers are part of fully operational, sophisticated businesses and groups. This is a trillion-dollar industry and requires highly specialized individuals to deliver.

Some of those specialties include:

- **Negotiators -** Because they have to get you to pay!
- **Access Brokers -** Who are highly specialized at the infiltration portion. They rely on the dark web's available credentials, phishing emails, and other network infiltration attempts to get in.
- **Technical Programmers -** Who can create highly scalable and automated systems to help deploy ransomware even faster.
- **Criminals -** Who rely on all of the above and just pay the money to have the infiltration, attacks, and negotiations take place on their behalf.

In this day and age, it's more important than ever to protect yourself from hackers. Businesses are becoming increasingly targeted, and it's important to know how to protect yourself and your data. In this chapter, we'll walk you through the steps you need to take to keep your data safe.

Cyber Risk Assessment (Analysis): Understand Your Data and Risk

Tell me, are you able to truly identify the data your company holds and the risk it presents to you and your clients?

Not only that but what processes do you have in place to protect that data?

As a business owner, you need to get started by understanding what is being stored, how it is being stored, and who has access to it. Only then can you truly assess what the severity of a cyber attack will look like. Yup, there will be costs to decrypt a ransomware attack if you don't have suitable backups in place, but what if the criminals were to take your data instead of just encrypting it and decide to sell it on the dark web?

Here is an example cost breakdown of a company that had roughly 5000 records exposed of either personal identifiable information (social insurance/security numbers, licenses, email addresses) or payment card industry information (credit cards):

Incident Investigation	
Breach Coach:	$50,000
Forensics:	$60,000
	$110,000
Notification and Crisis Management	
Crisis Management:	$30,000
Notification:	$8,800
Call Center:	$5,750
Credit Monitoring:	$4,500
	$49,050
Total Cost	**$159,050**

You can see these results for yourself using Breach Secure Now's free Breach Cost Calculator:

https://www.breachsecurenow.com/breach-cost-calculator/

Let me break down the above picture for you on what each of those costs is:

Breach Coach – This is the person or company your insurance is likely to hire to help you control the situation and plan for remediation. They will guide you through the rest of this process.

Forensics – The forensics team will investigate your company's systems and data from top to bottom to figure out just how bad the breach was, who was impacted, how it occurred, and what the next steps should be to remediate the breach.

Crisis Management – So you had a breach, all your data was not only encrypted but stolen and for sale on the dark web. Well, there are usually regulations in place to notify the public or media. This is where crisis management comes in to help avoid further reputational damage.

Notification – Remember all of that client data that was stolen? Well, you have to notify every client, usually by creating breach notification letters, advertisements, and web notifications.

Call Center – Depending on how big your breach was or your client base, you may need to temporarily set up a call center to handle incoming calls from individuals who were affected. They will have questions and expect timely answers.

Credit Monitoring – Credit monitoring services and/or identity monitoring services may be required for the individual's part of the breach. One more piece to help maintain your reputation.

So, you now understand your business's risk; let's talk about the pieces to put in place to protect that risk!

Educate Yourself and Your Employees

This is undeniably one of, if not the most, important things you can do as a business owner. Educate yourself, and educate your employees on cyber threats.

As mentioned in the story above, education on identifying and avoiding phishing scams is crucial for businesses to help keep their employees safe and data secure. There are great programs out there such as Breach Secure Now and Ninjio that make learning informative and entertaining, and keep your team up-to-date with current trends.

Technology changes rapidly. Always keep your employees up-to-date with monthly training, this isn't a one-and-done system. New attacks are created every day and the criminals are only getting smarter. The employees are the knights in your castle; let's give them some combat training.

Use Strong Passwords and Keep Them Safe

After employee training, password security is the next most important line of defence for stopping cyber criminals from accessing business owners' data.

Complexity requirements have increased and re-using the same passwords over and over again needs to be abandoned. We all have multiple places for which we have passwords within our businesses, ranging from a mere 1-10 pieces of software to some companies having up to 200 they use to accomplish their tasks. That is a **lot** of different logins to remember. This is where password managers come into play.

Password managers are a must-have for businesses. You would never just keep the key to your castle laying on the outside of the gate, would you? The key, or password in this case, needs to be put behind the walls, in a secure password manager. It lets the employees store their logins for the software they use and helps generate unique and complex passwords for every login—passwords they don't have to remember and may never even have to see. Programs like Keeper, which we use for our clients, allow you to share logins securely with permission-based folders, to the exact groups who need access.

Of course, passwords are just the first step to securing a login. They go hand-in-hand with our next, and by far, one of the most critical recommendations: multi-factor authentication.

Multi-Factor Authentication

So, your knight has a key (password) to your castle, but under all of that armour, are you sure you know who they truly are? You need MFA. Think of this second form of authentication as the knight shouting out the secret code, that was only good for that day (or 30 seconds in the real world).

Multi-factor authentication (MFA) is a security measure that requires users to provide more than one form of identification, such as a password, and a physical token to access their account. MFA is becoming increasingly popular among businesses because it increases the security of user accounts and data.

There are a few different ways to implement MFA in your business. Multi-factor authentication tools should send users an email, text, or authentication prompt on an app, or require using a hardware token before users can log in. Of course, this isn't to make life more difficult for everyone, but to ensure that the person who is inputting that password truly is who they say they are. The three methods I would like to focus on the most are SMS/text, authenticator app, and hardware token.

SMS and Text:

Of the three mentioned above, SMS is the least secure method. The reason is that cyber criminals can clone your SIM card and access your text messages that way. Additionally, mobile numbers can be paired with computers, so if the criminals have access to that computer, they could also send and receive text messages from it.

Authenticator App:

Another way to receive an MFA code is by using an authentication app on a mobile device. This eliminates the problem that text messages have with security. The only drawback is that it's a bit more of a setup, and if a mobile device is lost, there is the issue of resetting the MFA.

Physical Hardware Token:

The most secure way to receive your MFA code is by purchasing a security key device like YubiKey or Thetis. This key is not tied to a mobile number or mobile device that could be breached, and the user uses it to authentic-cate the MFA code by inserting it into a computer or mobile device. Losing the key is the only risk, but can be easily mitigated with employee training programs and procedures in the event of a lost key.

MFA is an important security measure, and businesses should implement it as soon as possible.

Install a Firewall (Physical or Software)

One of the most key parts of building a network is setting up some sort of firewall. Whether that is a traditional one, which consists of rack-mounted hardware installed in a network room, or a software-based firewall that runs directly on computers to provide protection.

If hackers are to be considered invaders, then a firewall would be your main gate. It's meant to be rigid, always online and only supposed to have certain traffic or data come through it. If you have loose security, it's basically like having an open invitation to all the neighboring bandits to come steal your info. This is exactly what you don't want to do.

On the flip side of that coin, you also don't want to impede the day-to-day workings of your business, aka, your castle. So, choosing what firewall you use and how you implement it is important. Some businesses may even consider using both a physical firewall as a gateway to the internet and a software firewall for an added layer of protection. It all depends on how you want to configure your network defence.

Traditional firewalls as mentioned are usually seen in the server room or network room of a business. Data traffic is allowed in based on what your IT team has chosen to block, where it's from, and/or what kind of data it is. Intrusion systems built into a firewall can also help determine if the data is bad, questionable, or safe. These kinds of firewalls are great for keeping traffic out and for monitoring traffic within your business.

Software-based firewalls are great for attaching a mobile security gate to your business computers. This kind of product is installed on all your machines and uses networking wizardry to mask your public internet address and filter any dangerous attacks coming in. Probably the coolest feature about this kind of firewall is that you can turn on "host isolation" which effectively hides your computer from the rest of the devices on the local network. This makes it very difficult for attackers to move about in your business and infect multiple machines. So even if someone does get through to one machine this will limit how widespread an attack will be.

Whatever you choose, choose wisely and make sure that the IT team who is implementing your firewall is considering all the angles of an attack, whether it's blocking outside attackers or protecting the devices from each other inside your network fortress. Picking a firewall is most certainly a critical part of protecting your business and your data.

Backing Up Your Data (Cloud and Onsite)

Many business owners are unaware of the importance of backing up their data. If your business is susceptible to a data breach, having a backup of your data can help you protect yourself from potential lawsuits and financial losses. There are several ways to back up your data, including using cloud-based backup services or storing your data onsite. My castle analogy has run dry on this one, as it is a bit hard to back up a whole castle without a human cloning feature.

At Rivercity Tech, we prefer to offer a two-pronged approach of both cloud and onsite (or near-site) backups.

Cloud Backups:

Cloud backups have taken off in the last decade. They allow for remote data storage, which makes it more accessible and secure at the same time. Being able to access the data from anywhere in the world at any time has been a huge advantage, especially with today's work-from-home growth. And of course, having cloud backups ensures peace of mind in the event of a data breach, corrupted data, or just accidentally deleting files.

Onsite Backups:

Having an onsite backup is also a great choice, and pairing it with a cloud backup is the best choice (in our opinion). With the same overall benefits mentioned in the cloud backups above, you also have the luxury of an extremely expedited recovery time in the event of a cyber attack where you need to recover all servers, VMs or files as fast as possible. The cloud can still do this, allowing for temporary virtual machines to be created — allowing your IT provider do some fancy routing changes while you wait to order a new server in — but onsite will do it quicker. (Of course, we recommend not having any physical severs onsite if you can help it.)

If you keep those backups regular, scheduled, and have routine checks to ensure recovery is possible, you will have a very efficient system in place.

Use antivirus and 24/7 threat hunting:

A no-brainer at this point, but antivirus is a must-have with any organization wanting to be serious about protecting their data from hackers. There are tons of different brands of antivirus out there ranging from home to business to enterprise usage levels. We recommend the business lines for our customers and ones that we can manage well. Brands like Microsoft Defender (our personal choice), Sentinel One, and Sophos are some of the bigger names in the industry. It is all fine and dandy to have antivirus on your computers, but without central management, it makes it hard to put policies in place.

An antivirus solution is the first line of computer defence, it's always on, scanning downloaded files, attachments and more, checking its database for millions of known vulnerabilities and reporting back. However, nowadays, antivirus is not enough, as sometimes ransomware can creep in, sit, wait, and strike when the time is right. That is where 24/7 threat hunting comes in.

This defence, 24/7 threat hunting, other times referred to as managed detection and response (MDR), is a solid partner for your antivirus. Most of the antivirus software you find will also have an optional MDR component, however.

At Rivercity Tech, we like to use Huntress as our MDR of choice. What it does for our clients is scan 24/7 for persistent footholds, that is, a hacker that has slipped through the back door undetected by abusing legitimate applications and processes. Once there, they establish a foothold and plan their attack, typically with ransomware or malware. Once Huntress has detected this foothold, their 24/7 team of real humans will put into place what is needed to eliminate these criminals from our clients' systems.

Together, we have a 24/7 security team always watching our clients and we highly recommend your current IT provider do the same for you.

So, as you can see, there are quite a few components needed to truly begin protecting your business data from cyber criminals. For more sensitive information, this is only the tip of the iceberg.

But listen, it's not all on you! That is why there are IT management consultants out there that specialize in cyber security and know exactly what your business needs to be fully protected (and compliant with your cyber insurance policy) like we do for our clients. Reach out to your local, trusted IT firm and ask for a cyber risk assessment. That is step one to understanding where you are at now, and which layers you need to add to be up to snuff. If you don't have a local IT firm or are looking for an outside opinion, you can always reach out to us at https://rivercitytech.ca/book-consultation.

If you mention this book and we find we are a good fit, we will perform your CSRA at 50% off.

About the Author

Mitch Redekopp is the CEO of Rivercity Technology Services Ltd. located in Saskatoon, Saskatchewan, Canada. In the past 7 years, Rivercity Tech has become known as one of the top Managed Services Providers in Saskatchewan, while also having a highly experienced Software Development department on hand.

Born and raised in Martensville, SK, Mitch quickly adopted a love for building computers, the ins, and outs of how they work, with a deep fascination for the interconnectivity of all thing's technology. Fast forward to today and nothing has changed. He is now the CEO of a business that has a deep focus on packaging together Cyber Security and creating bespoke solutions to help improve their client's internal business processes.

Mitch currently lives in Saskatoon with his wife and three children. He is an avid soccer (Manchester City), coffee and technology fan.

To schedule a Cyber Security Risk Assessment for your business, reach out to Mitch at www.rivercitytech.ca or email him directly at mitch@rivercitytech.ca

Data Privacy Regulations: 5 Things Your Business Must Know to Stay Compliant

By Rube Sayed

With the ever-increasing need for businesses to modernize their workplace and transform their businesses digitally, companies are required to ensure they abide by the data privacy regulations enforced by their state or country legislation. These data privacy regulations are being enforced locally and globally, and as a business owner, you are handling your data — and your client's data — in accordance with these best practices and standards. The challenge business owners face today is that there is no one single body that governs and mandates data privacy regulations globally in this ever-evolving digital landscape. As a business owner, you have access to numerous resources to ensure your business is protected; however, how do you know which data privacy regulations are relevant to you and how they apply to your business? The General Data Protection Regulation (GDPR) in Europe has shaped privacy regulations globally. Australia is regulated by the Australian Privacy Act (1988), and many privacy regulations in North and South America share legislation similar to that of the GDPR.

Datcom Cloud has been a managed IT and cyber security services provider in Sydney, Australia since 1997. Since its inception, we have acted for thousands of businesses as their outsourced IT department or an extension to their IT department as their virtual IT managers, CTOs, CIOs and CSIOs. We have the honor of helping law firms, finance and accounting practices, architectural and engineering firms, educational institutions, government business enterprises, and health and medical departments. Businesses usually reach out to us after experiencing a cyber security data breach or a compromise of their data that has caused significant outages, resulting in business disruption. Our incident response teams help get businesses back online with minimal downtime, data exposure, and data loss.

Using my decades of experience in designing, implementing, and managing IT environments of small-to-medium business enterprises, I have taken the liberty of summarizing and sharing the "5 Things Your Business Must Know to Stay Compliant" with the laws and regulations surrounding data privacy.

1. Data Compliance Assessment

The first and most important step towards honest data protection is to run some form of cyber security risk assessment or data protection assessment for your business. The assessments will enable you to identify and mitigate data protection risks and allow you to make informed decisions when planning to find a solution for those risks. Not only does it increase customer confidence by improving communication about data privacy risks, but it can also reduce the likelihood and cost of a disruption or breach. You can do this on your own using an online data protection assessment in accordance with your industry or region. For example, in the United States, companies can use an online tool.[9] Companies that are bound by GDPR may assess their compliance using the Data Protection Impact Assessment (DPIA).[10]

You can also engage your MSP or IT provider to run a cyber security risk assessment for your business. This will cost more, however, it is a much more detailed and holistic assessment to protect your business and ensure you make strategic decisions on managing the identified risk moving forward. In doing so, you can determine how susceptible your business is to an attack, examine how likely staff or employees are to enable or further the attack, identify physical and procedural weaknesses in the business that enable attacks, and identify the most likely business assets at risk.

A cyber security risk assessment is usually the first item we offer new clients. The reason is, it not only gives us insight into the business, but it also exposes your cyber security posture and how it stacks up to industry-leading best-practice methodologies. We urge businesses to immediately invest in basics such as multi-factor authentication (MFA), to reduce the ease of hackers infiltrating your network.[11]

The sad reality is, most clients approach us for our cyber security services after they have already experienced data loss or a cyber breach. They tend to ignore early warning signs, risking their compliance with privacy and data security laws. Customer data is critical to your business and it is sensitive to their business so you should be protecting it with the strongest measures possible. You owe it to your customers.

2. Professional Training

When a client provides you with their business data, it is well within their rights to want that data protected. Users play the most pivotal role in protecting their organization's data and stopping cyber breaches. Your business might have the most robust email and cyber security measures in place, but none of that matters if your business is not aware of the role it must play to alleviate human error. The majority of security breaches are a result of human error. It is simply not enough to assume all your staff — and even your clients — are aware of the importance surrounding data privacy and compliance.

It may seem like common sense, but research proves otherwise.[12] Some form of professional training, such as cyber security awareness training, must be implemented to reduce the risk to your business. Training can be online or face-to-face through an external company specializing in data compliance and should be undertaken annually at a minimum. As new staff are onboarded, it's a good idea to incorporate cyber security awareness training into their induction process.

We offer our employees as well as our clients cyber security awareness training which includes many topics that are relevant to Microsoft Office 365 security and compliance, as well as training in how to deal with impersonation fraud, ransomware, and phishing attacks. Because we are based in Australia, training and instruction comply with the Australian Privacy Act as well as GDPR, PCI, HIPAA, and most other data regulation laws.

Allow me to share one example highlighting why staff must be provided with cyber security awareness training:

A financial institution came to us after their employee opened an email and clicked on a link to a website. They were prompted to enter their credentials for what they believed was a legitimate website. They were unaware that their keystrokes were visible to the hacker, who, as a result, logged on to the systems and was able to infiltrate their network, encrypting all their data. Shortly thereafter, the company was unable to access any of its data. In most cases, the business would have the ability to restore from a cloud backup. However, to make matters worse, this client did not have offsite backup and their only backup was an external hard drive connected to the server, which was also encrypted. They were left in a vulnerable position, where they were ordered to pay a ransom of $2 million USD for their data. It is never recommended you pay a ransom, as it makes you a vulnerable target for future attacks by other hackers, and it is also no guarantee that you will get all your data back. There is also no guarantee that your data is not already up for sale on the dark web. In the end, we were able to salvage some data to get the company back in operation. Had this client prioritized some form of cyber security awareness training beforehand, it is possible this error could have been avoided.

This is only one story; I can list over one hundred similar stories of human error leading to cyber security breaches.

3. Engage a Lawyer

Data protection regulation in the context of increased online and cloud capacity breaches is a relatively new, technical, and evolving landscape. To ensure proper legal compliance and manage privacy risks for businesses and individuals alike, it is prudent to have access to compliance and legal personnel and/or resources. Interpretation of the regulations and implementation thereof will require the experts and business owners to work closely together to adopt and fine-tune such things as policies, legal documentation, and maintaining compliance. Proper accountability will stem from knowledge of the local and global data protection laws, but, essentially, legal advice on data protection applicable to the nature and functions of your organization and the jurisdiction in which it operates is crucial.

Since the implementation of the GDPR on May 25th, 2018, data protection requirements have been standardized across the EU and to some degree, US and Australian regulations are heading to closer alignment with the GDPR. To comply with the GDPR, any organization operating in the EU or doing business with individuals in the EU — regardless of the location of your business — must follow the data protection regulations of the GDPR.

This is particularly relevant due to the increase in online and cross-border business. Failure of organizations to comply can impose a maximum penalty of 4% of an organization's global turnover or up to 20 million EUR. Coupled with the damage and risk of data and privacy loss, sanctions against an organization for lack of adequate measures in place to offset and manage such losses are an added loss for organizations. Proper legal guidance and an internal framework are essential in navigating the landscape of data protection laws and implementing global and regional policies and practices.

Common to both the EU and Australia, legal compliance with data protection and management within an organization will involve carrying out the following functions:

- Identify the current compliance levels of the organization to the regulation applicable in the organization's jurisdiction
- Develop processing and compliance documentation and activities within the organization
- Educate employees on the importance and processing of privacy for personal information and protection
- Utilize resources as required: employees, outsourcing, legal, compliance, IT, security, and other experts
- Regularly maintain and review compliance with laws and processes, internally and externally

In effect, the GDPR governs businesses to be accountable for the following functions:

- By the implementation of privacy policies to protect and govern the privacy of employees and clients
- Appointment of a data protection officer to monitor personal data within the organization
- Conducting privacy impact statement
- Keeping records of processing activities
- Protecting personal data by default and by design
- Implementing security measures
- Liability of third parties
- Transparency of use and collection of personal information
- Breach notification
- Clear and specific consent requests for the free collection of information, including for minors

In Australia, the main obligations imposed by the law for the collection and protection of personal information are set out in the 13 Australian Privacy Principles (APP):[13]

- APP entities must manage personal information in an open and transparent way

- APP entities must give individuals the option of not identifying themselves
- APP entities can collect personal information and sensitive information in accordance with standards
- APP entities must deal with unsolicited personal information in a specific way
- An APP entity that collects personal information about an individual must take reasonable steps either to notify the individual of certain matters or to ensure the individual is aware of those matters
- APP entities can only use or disclose personal information for a purpose for which it was collected
- An organization must not use or disclose personal information it holds for direct marketing unless an exception applies
- Before an APP entity discloses personal information to an overseas recipient, the entity must take reasonable steps to ensure that the overseas recipient does not breach the APPs in relation to the information
- An organization must not adopt, use, or disclose a government-related identifier unless an exception applies

- An APP entity must take reasonable steps to ensure that the personal information it collects is accurate, up-to-date, and complete
- An APP entity must take reasonable steps to destroy or de-identify the personal information it holds once the personal information is no longer needed for the purpose for which the personal information may be used or disclosed under the APPs
- An APP that holds personal information about an individual must give the individual access to that information on request
- An APP entity must take reasonable steps to correct personal information to ensure that it is accurate, up-to-date, relevant, and not misleading[14].

Unlike the GDPR, the designation of a data privacy/ protection officer is not mandatory but recommended by the Australian privacy regulator, The Office of the Australian Information Commissioner (OAIC). The OAIC is also responsible for handling notifiable breaches in data.[15]

4. Reporting a Data Breach

It is likely that sometime in your career, there will come a time when you might encounter a situation involving a data breach. According to the OAIC, a data breach occurs when personal information held by an organization is lost or subjected to unauthorized access or disclosure.

For example, when:

- A device or paper record containing a customer's personal information is lost or stolen
- A database with personal information is accessed in an unauthorized manner
- Personal information is disclosed to the wrong person by error or by unauthorized means

Following a suspected breach of protected information, the organization must quickly assess the situation to determine if it is likely to cause serious harm to any individual. If so, it is essential to first notify the affected individuals, the information commissioner in your region, and in some major cases the media. In Australia, we have the Australian Notifiable Data Breaches (NDB) scheme in accordance with the Australian Privacy Act, which outlines that breaches must be reported to the OAIC. In the UK, data breaches are reported to the Information Commissioner's Office (ICO) in compliance with the GDPR.[16] Each country or region will have its own body that handles notifiable data breaches, so be sure to know which applies to your organization.

It's common for organizations or businesses to feel unsure about whether a breach has occurred. My advice is, if you're unsure, make contact with the commissioner's office for your region and ask. It is always better to be safe than sorry. If you are in the UK, you can perform an online self-assessment which will advise you of your next steps.[17]

5. Cloud Computing

It is no secret why more and more businesses are shifting to cloud computing; it's flexible, allows you to work remotely from any device, is more time- and cost-efficient, and better for the environment. Disaster recovery and data security are other major reasons that organizations, specifically small businesses, are making the move to the cloud. An increasing 83% of IT leaders trust cloud services as shown in a survey performed by Salesforce.[18]

Technology and security are only going to grow more solid as time passes, however, all businesses should still do their part to ensure their data is stored safely and in compliance with applicable laws. So how is an enterprise expected to do this when the location of the cloud data is very difficult to pinpoint to a specific geographic location? The data is constantly being transferred from one location to another or might reside in multiple locations. It is recommended that if a cloud provider operates in many jurisdictions, best to try to negotiate a tailored contract with your provider. You want ownership of your data, access to retrieve your data, and immediate notification of data breaches, so protocols and clauses must be included in service agreements with providers, in accordance with the geographically relevant laws.[19]

Most of my clients will specify the region they wish their data to reside. The majority of public cloud providers will have global regions and provide data residency options to bring your apps closer to your users. As a client, you own the data, and you can be in control of which geographic location you wish to deploy that data. Cloud providers might offer you the option to copy your data within a given geography for data redundancy or other operational purposes. Geo-redundancy allows you to reside your data between two regions to enhance the data durability in the case of a major data center disaster. For example, in Australia, you could choose the Australia East data center region in New South Wales and/or the Australia South East region in Victoria to house your data. I believe it is best practice to invest in geo-redundancy to ensure you are safeguarded from possible data loss should a data center face a disaster.

Essentially, when you engage with a cloud provider, you are trusting and relying upon the controls they have in place to ensure your data is secure in the cloud. It is important to assess the level of IT security measures or certifications the provider has implemented. You can do this via a risk assessment process performed by the DPIA. You have every right to audit your provider, so, regardless, this needs to be included in your service contract. Otherwise, according to an article released by Deloitte,[20] cloud providers can demonstrate their compliance with security and privacy laws through certifications such as the ISO 27001 (information security management system) or ISO 27018 (code of practice for protection of personally identifiable information (PII) in public clouds acting as PII processors).

These certifications are quite difficult to obtain and most MSPs will not have these certifications. This is not an issue, as long as the cloud your data is stored in is ISO 27001 and 27018 certified. This will ensure your data is most secure and your business is compliant with applicable data privacy regulations.

I can guarantee you peace-of-mind, minimal downtime, reduced disruptions, and even a competitive advantage should you follow and/or implement the advice above. We are living in uncertain and scary times, be it a pandemic or rising geographical tensions, so I encourage you to review the cyber security measures you have in place and educate yourself and your employees on ways to mitigate potential cyber threats. No amount of legislation can protect your business, you have to step up and take control of what is yours. Don't be discouraged to ask for professional advice, we all need help or a simple nudge in the right direction sometimes, it will only make you better and more knowledgeable. As a business owner, you're responsible for protecting your customer's data — no matter where you are and what jurisdiction you fall under, it is the law.

Visit our website at Datcom.com.au and contact me for advice on how we can help your business protect its data.

About the Author

Rube Sayed is the General Manager of Datcom Cloud, a family-owned, Managed ICT Services firm in Sydney, Australia, specialising in Cyber-security, Cloud Computing, Modern Workspace, Digital Transformation and Unified Communications.

Rube completed a Bachelor of Science in Information Technology and a Diploma in Information Technology at the University of Technology, Sydney and has since added over 50 technology certifications across 25 years of experience working with the world's leading technologies. Rube is an innovative leader in the field, a multiple winner of the Top Performing Partner Representative award and two-time winner of the Highest Growth ServiceONE Partner award issued by Hewlett Packard Enterprise. Rube lives in Sydney, Australia with his wife and two children.

Book your complimentary Cybersecurity Risk Assessment with Rube on

https://datcom.com.au/rube/.

What Is a Zero-Day Attack?

By John Kumley

On January 6th, 2021, servers across the globe responsible for sending, delivering, and storing email (exchange servers) were attacked. A Chinese espionage group known as "HAFNIUM" shared with the world a simple way to compromise these servers previously thought to be secure. HAFNIUM was known for targeting various United States government servers. They would then upload the breached data onto websites that others could access. Hackers were able to use this vulnerability to access servers to steal information. Hundreds of thousands of organizations were affected, including small businesses, cities, and the United States government. There were no patches or fixes for this vulnerability until March 2nd of that year. All organizations that had exchange servers had to assume that all of their email communications had been pillaged. Organizations throughout the world had to migrate to Microsoft's Exchange Online service, an email service not affected by this attack. Because this computer software vulnerability was unknown and there was no known patch to correct it, this incident is known as a Zero Day Attack.

There is a series of steps a hacker would need to complete to pull off a successful breach of these systems. The first step is to identify an impactful target: hackers look to attack pieces of software that have a large number of users. For example, this could be a browser such as Google Chrome or your Amazon Echo device controlling your home. When choosing a target, the hacker will most likely not be aware of any vulnerabilities in this piece of software so failure can be a very probable outcome. Large software companies invest millions of dollars by employing the best security professionals the world has to offer to keep users like you safe from exploits. Hackers take a risk with the possibilities of months of work to find a vulnerability in this software. This is a risk they take in order to reap their personal rewards.

The second step is called resonance: during this time, hackers research everything remotely relevant and related to their target. Their goal is to build up a massive documentation resource to answer questions about the target software and its ecosystem. Using this information, hackers learn about the target's security history, seeing if there are any previous or existing exploits that they may be able to use. Many of these pieces of software have millions of lines of code. Hackers need to use this resonance to narrow down the amount of information they will need to review. Generally, they find historically bad components to exploit. Quite often, this code has only been lightly patched and there are still vulnerabilities until the code is rewritten. The bad code used in this exploit was most likely written by a novice developer with little oversight and as a small project to support the larger ones. Once the target code is identified, the hackers begin the third step of "bug hunting." Hackers use sophisticated techniques to test attacks and break the blocks of code. After testing, hackers find a bug that would allow them to secretly execute code. Once the hacker has found this exploit in the software, they are faced with several choices: they can report this bug to the software vendor, they can cloud sell it to a broker who will then sell this exploit to the highest bidder, or they can continue the attack themselves. The attacker uses this exploit to create a perfect program, process, and payload that they soon launch towards the target software. Hackers who now have access to systems though this zero-day exploit have a chance to get what they came for and allow others to soon do the same.

Soon after this vulnerability in the target system is exposed, antivirus signatures are released. Antivirus vendors work hard to identify the malware and update their antivirus to block the malware from reaching the attacked systems. During this time, systems could still be exposed because a proper patch is not yet released for the software. Developers work diligently to release a patch for the breached systems; this could take any time from hours to months before the patch has finished development. And when the patch is released, users may not take initiative to deploy it. Organizations may not have patch management policies in place or users may just simply ignore their updates whenever possible, which will keep them vulnerable. When a user or organization removes the malware from their systems, patching their affected software, the zero-day attack is over. But the effects of the attack may last for many years to come.

Zero-day attacks are difficult to thwart. But there are a number of effective best practices to help remove or prevent a zero-day attack from affecting your organization.

1. Patch Management and Deployment Policy

All organizations should have a developed patch management policy for their devices and software. Whenever a patch is released to increase security or to patch a known vulnerability, organizations need a policy that they can follow to ensure that they regularly implement patches on their systems. Larger organizations will need to have engineers regularly evaluate patches, manage, and automate deployment of patches. Patch management cannot stop a zero-day attack, but it can make sure that when the patch is released that your system's exposure will be limited.

2. Windows Defender Exploit Guard

Windows Defender is an antimalware software built into recent versions of Microsoft Windows. If you have Windows 10 or higher, you will have some version of Windows Defender installed. One of its components, named Exploit Guard, protects users from zero-day attacks. Exploit Guard can be broken up into four components: Windows Defender Smart Screen protects the endpoint against any internet-based threats by blocking any programs on the computer from being sent to untrusted hosts or IP addresses. Attack Surface Reduction (ASR) seamlessly blocks malware from entering the machine through Microsoft Office email and script-based malware. Controlled Folder Access offers protection for your computer by prohibiting changes to system-critical folders from untheorized programs. And finally, exploit protection offers a full suite of vulnerability elimination techniques directly built into windows.

3. Next-Generation Antivirus (NGAV)

NGAV is for organizations that need the ability to block zero-day threats that are currently unknown. This advanced endpoint protection uses static and behavioral AI to respond intelligently against cyber threats. NGAV will analyze all the programs and processes on your machine. When a threat is detected, the antivirus will track, respond, and reverse the impact of cyber attacks. Security teams will autonomously review the data of the attack and report to the software vendor affected.

4. Advanced Endpoint Firewall (WAF)

In 2020, the COVID-19 virus impacted how many organizations physically placed their workers. Most employers gave their employees the option to work from home. These employees were no longer protected by server rooms full of security and firewalls. It soon became very clear that employers needed to provide the same level or greater protection as in the office setting so that users could work anywhere securely. Endpoint WAF isolates devices from the public network and makes them invisible in coffee shops or your home network. This firewall that lives on your device will verify your user and limit access to only authorized resources. And with an intrusion prevention system that analyzes all the network traffic to prevent vulnerability exploits, endpoint firewall replaces many large firewall appliances in today's market.

5. Incident Response Plan

Organizations of any size should implement an incident response plan that delivers an organized process for detection and response to cyber attacks, including zero-days. Having a well put together plan will minimalize confusion and increase your chances of preventing or reducing the impact of a cyber attack. When writing your plan, you should follow SANS Institute's six steps in handling a computer incident:

- Preparation: during this phase, you would perform a risk assessment to identify your most vulnerable/sensitive areas. This section of the document should include documentation of processes for communication of any sensitive information across the organization.

- Identification: you should define how your organization plans to identify a zero-day threat. Many of the tools spoken of earlier in this chapter will enable you to identify and report to your security team. The identification process will also state what further data needs to be gathered to deal with the attack.

- Containment: after you have identified a security incident, you must define the immediate and long-term steps that need to be executed to prevent further damage and/or exposure to your systems and data. This process is known as containment.

- Eradication: during this phase, you will identify and remove the root cause of the attack. Steps will be taken to document this incident thoroughly and ensure that an attack cannot happen again.

- Recovery: a documented process on how to bring systems online and assess them to confirm they are back to security standards.

- Lessons learned: within two weeks of recovery, your security officer should compile all the data related to the incident. Your organization may be required to report this data — for instance, organizations that are under HIPPA law. Once the Who, What, Where, Why, and How questions are answered, the incident report is finished.

I hope I have illustrated the importance of protecting yourself from zero-day attacks. Overcoming zero-day attacks can be a nightmare for any sized organization. But by following best practices, having a well-built security software stack, and a plan of action, you can minimalize impact for your organization. Software vendors invest very heavily in their security, along with offering prizes to individuals that discover vulnerabilities and report them.

Do you have an IT Department or service provider to ensure you are protected from attacks? My company, Pacific Cloud IT, is a cyber security-focused IT support provider. Our focus is to give your organization a complete, multi-layer defense against incoming cyber threats. If we can be of any help, please reach out and we would be happy to help you or your organization.

About the Author

At an early age, John Kumley worked with any computer system he could get his hands on. Growing up, John offered technical support to all of his friends and family. In 2014, John founded a computer repair and support company called Technical Genius Solutions LLC.

Over the years, he grew the business and managed local businesses and municipalities until he eventually sold the business in 2021. In 2021, John founded Pacific Cloud IT Inc., focusing on businesses with 10-49 employees. Pacific Cloud IT offers a refined cyber security solution and IT services based on industry best practices and a deep commitment to quality. PCIT recognizes cyber attacks can wound or kill any company, and understands the stress business owners feel. Our vision and communication skills are as important as our technical prowess when engaging with clients.

When not working, John spends his time traveling around the globe, hiking and paddleboarding where wonder is to be found.

Pacific Cloud IT

(503) 449 2009

www.Pacificcloudit.com

The Most Common Cyber Attacks

By A. Samuel Disraelly

As a small business owner, there are two things to understand early on about cyber security.

The most dangerous time for a computer isn't the first five minutes it's connected to the internet, though experts say an IoT device or computer can get infected that quickly. No. The most likely time a computer will be breached or infected with some kind of malware is when a human sits at the keyboard of a computer.

Once a small business owner can recognize what makes their computers most vulnerable, the next step is to understand the most effective tool in protecting them. The most important protection is not the latest in endpoint detection and response. It isn't a security or network operations center either. It's not even a strong, corporate-grade antivirus. The most important tool in keeping computers safe, the people in an organization productive, and data secure is... education.

The more a person knows, the more they learn, and the more they surround themselves and their organization with a team of dedicated, knowledgeable professionals, the better these IT professionals can keep their clients safe and working, for the betterment of that organization.

With that in mind, this chapter will discuss some key points to learn about the different kinds of cyber attacks that occur these days, and how they can affect a business.

For this purpose, we'll break down the method of attacks into three categories:

1. Attacks on Data
2. Attacks on Infrastructure
3. Attacks on Money or Employees

Attacks on Data

The most common types of attacks we hear about these days on the news or social media is ransomware.

There are three different ways a hacker can attempt to extort money if they get access to systems and data.

Access Ransom, Extortion Ransom, and Extortion of a Client Base.

Ransomware is an attack, most commonly run by some kind of malware on a computer, that often will start by encrypting files on the computers, systems, and network. This leaves users and organizations without access to key data and applications. The victim's computer will be left barely functioning and useless. Think of this like kidnapping. This is what we call *access ransom*. The victim will not have access to their machine, systems or data until the ransom is paid or recovered through other methods.

An attack of this nature will often be accompanied by a ransom letter, informing the target of what has happened and providing some method of payment, promising that the victim will receive a decryption key or program after payment is made. The Colonial Pipeline attack of 2021 was a case of access ransom. But this is only how it starts.

Often, before the encryption is performed on the machine in question, the data on the system will be uploaded to the attacker. This will allow them to review the data and do with it as they will. This is called *extortion ransom*. It's not about denial of access to the company systems, it's about extorting money from the target based on control over the data.

Even if the target of such an attack recovers and gets their systems running again — either by paying the ransom, by restoring backups, or by any other method — the perpetrators still have potentially valuable data from the target. They may approach the owner of the data, asking them to pay the hackers not to release the data on the dark web, they may use it themselves, or they may contact the victim's clients to convince them that the company has been compromised and should no longer be a trusted vendor.

Beyond that, there is the potential for what is called *extortion of the client base*. The perpetrators could still contact the clients of the company that was hit and ask those clients to pay. If those clients choose not to pay, the data or personal information that pertains to them discovered during the attack may be disclosed on the dark web.

The Ashley Madison/Avid Life Media data breach of 2015 was an example of two kinds of extortion attacks on data. First, the original perpetrators of the attack approached the company and told them to shut down operations or their data would be released. When the company didn't terminate the website, the data was released. News outlets later did stories on accounts with email addresses related to countries where adultery is punishable by death, like Saudi Arabia. News outlets also reported that extortionists focused on .mil and .gov addresses, where military and government officials could suffer damage to their family lives and careers by being linked to adulterous activities.

Beyond Ransomware and Attacks on Data, there are Attacks on Infrastructure

Cyber attacks can affect a company's productivity. One of the more common attacks is a DOS or DDOS attack. This stands for *Denial of Service* or *Distributed Denial of Service*. These attacks flood a network or systems with so much traffic that legitimate services can't get through. Think of a radio being "jammed." There is so much static that no legitimate traffic can get through. Computers talk to other computers and the rest of the internet through a simple wire in the back. If they get bombarded with communication requests from illegitimate sources, this could clog up the network so that no legitimate traffic can get through. In 2020, two of the largest companies on the Internet were both hit and affected by DDOS attacks. Google was hit in October... but more notably, for three days in February, Amazon's Web Services (AWS), which potentially powers up to half of the internet, was hit with one of the largest and most effective DDOS attacks on record. Personally, we saw SAAS applications go down, and several Voice Over IP providers affected, causing disruptions to businesses that were not directly engaging AWS. These small businesses had never heard of AWS, but they were adversely affected for days with phones that either wouldn't ring or call out.

While DDOS attacks can affect a network, there are tons of other kinds of attacks that will affect the productivity of computers and systems.

The large umbrella of malware, defined as any software made for malicious purposes or interfering with a computer's normal functioning, covers a wide variety of dangerous software that affects the usability of a user's system. Trojans and viruses with destructive payloads can destroy data or systems, affecting productivity. Spyware and keyloggers can be used to steal credentials and other data. Worms and bots can be used to spread malware or malicious code, and control or utilize computers and systems for nefarious outcomes.

Another attack that's on the rise is cryptojacking: running software on a machine that utilizes clock cycles to mine cryptocurrencies and sends them back to an attacker who does not own the machine or pay for the power consumed to run it. Often, the only thing a user that has been hit with a cryptojacking will notice is a slightly slower machine, or higher heat generation. These attacks are more successful the longer they stay undetected. In 2021, Microsoft found vulnerabilities in its Exchange Server software that made it specifically susceptible to remote code execution that was being used in cryptojacking attacks. A mail server that is on all the time without people commonly sitting at it, gauging its speed and responsiveness, would be an ideal target for this kind of attack. While not particularly destructive or disruptive, these could be highly profitable for a perpetrator.

And as we discussed with ransomware, rarely is one attack or malicious activity found alone on a machine. Combinations of attacks are used to make sure the effect spreads from machine to machine, network to network, so something that starts with a single machine can grow to affect large swaths of the internet.

Attacks on Money or Employees

Once we've looked at the attacks on our hardware and infrastructure, and attacks on the data, we now look at **attacks on people**. As said before, the weakest point in a company's cyber defense armor is the human behind the keyboard. That attack on the human leads to other attacks, on company finances, credentials, and other services.

Three leading types of these attacks are:

- BEC (business email compromise)
- Phishing
- MITM (man in the middle)

Business email compromise is so pervasive that the FBI has a specific page on its website just to educate about it. Examples of business email compromise could be as simple and innocuous as a vendor sending a bookkeeping department an invoice with a notice of "new mailing address". It could also look like a CEO asking an employee to run out and grab a bunch of gift cards as last minute "Thank You" gifts for clients and vendors before the holiday season. The stories are everywhere. Business email compromise is a type of phishing campaign that tends to focus on a payoff in financial results for the attacker — getting a check in the mail, gift card serial numbers, or a wire transfer.

Other types of phishing attacks can be about malware distribution and infection, or can tend to focus on data and credential acquisition.

Some of the most common phishing attacks are paired with attachments — PDF or Word docs attached to emails, like a resume sent to an HR director or an invoice sent to a bookkeeper. Executable code can run when PDFs are opened in Adobe. Macros may run when an infected Word document is opened, or when an .EXE executable attachment or downloadable link is clicked from a legitimate-looking call-to-action in an email.

This is why the set of protective tools we offer our clients and customers includes not just one but at least two layers of protection for email — both at the perimeter (before email even touches the server), and live email monitoring on the server. These keep you up-to-date and protected from zero day attacks.

Sometimes phishing attacks look like an email from Amazon or Walmart alerting a person to an order recently placed on their account that they didn't expect. It could also be a notification from a bank that there was a transaction that isn't recognized. These kinds of phishing attacks can be paired and lead into man in middle attacks or credential theft/fake login pages.

Man in the middle (MITM) attacks are when someone attempts to put themselves between a user and a legitimate service; they attempt to impersonate that service to gain credentials to that service.

We have seen some great examples of MITM attacks. There were reports in the press in 2013 that some government actors have impersonated Google with fake search pages that would allow them to collect data about what people were searching for online. Router companies have used MITM processes to redirect users to products made by that same company when searching online for technology products. Some internet service providers use this kind of technology to inject code and replace ads on websites that their users visit with ads that are under their control.

Credential theft/fake login pages are everywhere online also. Last year, a hacker paid Google to place ads to their fake bank login site for a bank. By paying for ads, that link appeared above the "organic" and legitimate links to the bank's actual website. A security specialist in our office actually clicked on the fake link and found themselves looking at a fake site, designed to steal credentials. We contacted the bank and let them know someone was impersonating them, but what could they do?

We tried reaching out to Google to let them know they were being used in an attack but were unable to contact a live person with any ability to help. With a little research, we were able to determine that the fake login page was hosted on the webserver that belonged to a paid parking structure near LAX airport. We contacted them, told them their site had been hacked, and that the hacker was using it as a link in a chain attempting to steal credentials. We were able to point out the directory the bad page was hidden under, and the manager got ahold of the owner, and the owner got ahold of the webmaster. As a result, within 45 minutes of our team noticing the page, it was taken down, and the link in a chain that could have led to hundreds if not thousands of bank users falling for this attack, was broken.

More recently, our team identified another similar attack. A client received a spam phishing email that prompted the user to click on a link that went to a page hosted on a normally legitimate web hosting service. That link led to another website with a name similar to "oneshareddriveonline," a site that could be misconstrued as being a site similar to Microsoft's OneDrive. The site even showed the OneDrive logo and offered multiple methods of logging in: Outlook, Yahoo, AOL, etc. In this case, however, our team notified both webhosts: the host of the target of the link in the emails, and the host of the fake login page. Unfortunately, two weeks later, the chain remains unbroken and is still capturing people's credentials. This is the perfect example of ambivalence and complacency being the biggest opponents to security.

These are not isolated incidents. In 2020, email security firm IRONSCALES logged more than 50,000 fake login pages pretending to be over 200 brands worldwide. The firm identified emails that linked to as many as 11,000 fake PayPal login sites, over 9,000 fake Microsoft login pages, 7,500 fake Facebook login pages, and fake login pages for other key brands and sites like eBay, Amazon, Gap, LinkedIn, banks, airlines, and credit card companies.

In summary, the methods of attack are as varied as the people behind them. They can be mixed and matched. They can be disruptive, or maybe even slip by for days or weeks undetected.

But all these types of attacks can be avoided and defended against.

How?

First, recognize the biggest potential for a breach in security starts with the human element. Then remember the two best defenses against compromises starts with user education and having a well-trained, responsive cyber security and support team engaged and at your disposal.

For example, at our company, Your Tech Department, we say, "Every business, no matter how big or how small, deserves a Tech Department. Let us be yours!" And there's a reason for that. Our clients, when they have us engaged in regular, unlimited support contracts, don't hesitate to pick up the phone and ask us to remote in and "look at something funny that just popped up on a screen." That 30-second phone call or two-minute remote session can save days of downtime and thousands of dollars of lost revenue or productivity. So, it's important to make sure you have that team in place. You also want to make sure you're on a security services plan that monitors email, makes sure passwords aren't being reused, networks are being monitored and endpoints are protected, managed, and patched.

Educate yourself and your team with security awareness training and test their knowledge with regular test phishing campaigns. Be mindful of security at all times. It only takes a minute to think twice before clicking on something you don't recognize.

A business owner doesn't have to be scared... you don't have to throw your computer out the window and go back to pen and paper for all things. You can be safe on the Internet, but it will help to have trained professionals available and engaged, supporting your team.

For more information on the topics discussed in this chapter, please check out: http://book.YourTech.co

Also, if you'd like to hear more about how we can help keep you safe as you run your business on the Internet, or if you decide you'd like us to be Your Tech Department, find us online at: http://book.YourTech.co or call 203-883-0000.

About the Author

A. Samuel Disraelly has always been surrounded by technology. The son of two computer consultants who were part of the first generation of computer programmers, he was given an Apple 2 as his first computer at the age of 5.

Mr. Disraelly is founder and partner of Your Tech Department, LLC, a technology consulting firm and provider of managed services that has served hundreds of clients from the Northeastern Region of the U.S. to across the globe for almost 15 years. Over the years, Your Tech has expanded with subsidiaries to create the Your Tech Life family of companies, providing VOIP, Internet, Smart Home, and Cyber Security Services.

Along with serving small businesses, he has freelanced for large enterprise companies like Acxiom, Polk, Equifax, Clairol, William Pitt Sotheby's International Realty, and others.

He has spent years supporting clients through all kinds of technology needs, watching markets and industries, and always tries to stay ahead of the curve. He has spent the last few years focusing on Cyber Security for his clients.

He holds multiple degrees and certifications in Technical and Computer Studies, Liberal Arts and General Studies.

His experience with technology is tempered by a family instilled desire to serve the community. He joined the Navy at 17 and has held certifications and served in numerous public safety positions including CPR & Lifeguard Instructor, Firefighter, Rescue Diver and 911 Operator. He served the Connecticut State Legislature as Assistant Clerk to the Judiciary Committee. He served eight years as an elected Constable for the City of Norwalk and is currently serving on numerous boards and public service organizations.

Academic and professional distinctions include Coca-Cola New Century Scholar, Connecticut All-State Academic Team and nominated to the USA Today All Academic Team. He served two years as a member of the Board of Trustees for the Connecticut State Community College system. He served one year as International Vice President for Phi Theta Kappa, International Honor Society for Two-Year Schools. He has spoken and guest lectured on Life, Technology and Ethics across the country.

He lives in Connecticut with his wife, Elaine, their two young girls, Rebecca and Katarina, and their amazing dog, Carson.

Ari Sam can be reached via:

Your Tech Department, LLC
Phone: 203.883.0000
EMail: sam@yourtech.co
Web: http://book.yourtech.co

End Notes

[1] https://cybersecurityventures.com/cybercrime-damages-6-trillion-by-2021

[2] Spoofing: A type of scam in which a criminal disguises an email address, display a name, phone number, text message, or website URL to convince a target that they are interacting with a known, trusted source. Spoofing often involves changing just one letter, number, or symbol of the communication so that it looks valid at a quick glance. For example, you could receive an email that appears to be from Netflix using the fake domain name "netffix.com." (Source: https://www.investopedia.com/terms/s/spoofing.asp)

[3] Clickjacking: An attack that tricks a user into clicking a webpage element which is invisible or disguised as another element. This can cause users to unwittingly download malware, visit malicious web pages, provide credentials or sensitive information, transfer money, or purchase products online.
(Source: https://www.imperva.com/learn/application-security/clickjacking)

[4] Sniffing: Often people confuse spoofing with a sniffing attack. The terms sniffing and spoofing are frequently used interchangeably. However, sniffing is different from spoofing attacks. Sniffing includes the attacker's direct involvement with the target. They intercept network traffic to listen for and read unencrypted data actively. On the other hand, spoofing attacks are man-in-the-middle attacks in which the attacker impersonates another person. They intercept data passing between the targets and the network to gain access to sensitive information. (Source: https://cisomag.eccouncil.org/what-are-sniffing-attacks-and-how-to-defend-against-them)

[5] https://cybersecurityventures.com/hackerpocalypse-cybercrime-report-2016/

[6] https://news.gallup.com/poll/355907/remote-work-persisting-trending-permanent.aspx

[7] https://nvlpubs.nist.gov/nistpubs/specialpublications/nist.sp.800-46r2.pdf

[8] https://www.cisa.gov/publication/cisa-cyber-essentials

[9] HIPAA Journal. (2014-2022). HIPAA Risk Assessment. Retrieved from HIPAA Journal: https://www.hipaajournal.com/hipaa-risk-assessment/

[10] Wolford, B. (2022). Data Protection Impact Assessment (DPIA). Retrieved from GDPR.EU: https://gdpr.eu/data-protection-impact-assessment-template

[11] Datcom. (2021). IT Support for your Business. Retrieved from Datcom: https://datcom.com.au

[12] Mimecast. (2003-2022). Cyber Awareness Training. Retrieved from Mimecast: https://www.mimecast.com/content/cyber-security-awareness-training/

[13] Fitzgerald, L. (2021, May). Guide to data protection in Australia. Retrieved from Lander & Rodger: https://www.landers.com.au/legal-insights-news/terralex-guide-to-data-protection-2021

[14] Fitzgerald, L. (2021, May). Guide to data protection in Australia. Retrieved from Lander & Rodger: https://www.landers.com.au/legal-insights-news/terralex-guide-to-data-protection-2021

[15] Office of the Australian Information Commissioner (OAIC). (2022). Office of the Australian Information Commissioner (OAIC). Retrieved from Office of the Australian Information Commissioner (OAIC): https://www.oaic.gov.au

[16] Information Commissioner's Office (ICO). (2022). Report a breach. Retrieved from Information Commissioner's Office (ICO): https://ico.org.uk/for-organisations/report-a-breach/

[17] Information Commissioner's Office (ICO). (2022). Self-Assessment for Data Breaches.

[18] Salesforce. (2020, October 1). What are the Advantages of Cloud Computing? 10 Reasons to Move to the Cloud. Retrieved from Salesforce Blog: https://www.salesforce.com/uk/blog/2015/11/why-move-to-the-cloud-10-benefits-of-cloud-computing.html

[19] Tolsma, A. (2022). GDPR and the impact on cloud computing. Retrieved from Deloitte:
https://www2.deloitte.com/nl/nl/pages/risk/articles/cyber-security-privacy-gdpr-update-the-impact-on-cloud-computing.html

[20] Ibid.

Made in United States
Orlando, FL
10 November 2026

90498884R00115